Warrior • 62

OSPREY
PUBLISHING

# Prussian Regular Infantryman 1808–15

Oliver Schmidt • Illustrated by Steve Noon

First published in Great Britain in 2003 by Osprey Publishing, Elms Court, Chapel Way, Botley, Oxford OX2 9LP, United Kingdom.
Email: info@ospreypublishing.com

© 2003 Osprey Publishing Ltd.

All rights reserved. Apart from any fair dealing for the purpose of private study, research, criticism or review, as permitted under the Copyright, Designs and Patents Act, 1988, no part of this publication may be reproduced, stored in a retrieval system, or transmitted in any form or by any means, electronic, electrical, chemical, mechanical, optical, photocopying, recording or otherwise, without the prior written permission of the copyright owner. Enquiries should be addressed to the Publishers.

A CIP catalogue record for this book is available from the British Library.

ISBN 1 84176 056 0

Editor: Thomas Lowres
Design: Ken Vail Graphic Design, Cambridge, UK
Index by David Worthington
Originated by Grasmere Digital Imaging, Leeds, UK
Printed in China through World Print Ltd.

03 04 05 06 07   10 9 8 7 6 5 4 3 2 1

FOR A CATALOGUE OF ALL BOOKS PUBLISHED BY OSPREY MILITARY AND AVIATION PLEASE CONTACT:

Osprey Direct UK, P.O. Box 140, Wellingborough, Northants, NN8 2FA, UK
E-mail: info@ospreydirect.co.uk

Osprey Direct USA, c/o MBI Publishing, P.O. Box 1, 729 Prospect Ave, Osceola, WI 54020, USA
E-mail: info@ospreydirectusa.com

www.ospreypublishing.com

## Artist's note

Readers may care to note that the original paintings from which the colour plates in this book were prepared are available for private sale. All reproduction copyright whatsoever is retained by the Publishers. All enquiries should be addressed to:

Steve Noon,
50 Colchester Avenue,
Penylan,
Cardiff,
CF23 9BP

The Publishers regret that they can enter into no correspondence upon this matter.

## Author's note

In memory of Sabina Hermes.

All images not sourced can be credited to the author's own collection.

## Acknowledgements

I wish to express my thanks to the following people: Frank Bader, Günter Berker, John Cook, Michael Czaika, Dallas Gavan, Peter Seifert, Lars-Holger Thümmler, Bernd Windsheimer, Jakob Ziegert, Bruno Dreier (Blüchermuseum Kaub) and Joachim Niemeyer (WGM Rastatt).

FRONT COVER **Combat at Lüneburg on 2 April 1813, by Richard Knötel. When skirmishers of the *Füsilier-Bataillon* of the *1. Pommersches Infanterie-Regiment* had fired all their ammunition, Johanna Stegen, a girl from the town, ran to the battalion's ammuniton carriage and, in the midst of enemy fire, distributed new cartridges to them.**

# CONTENTS

# PRUSSIAN REGULAR INFANTRYMAN 1808–15

## INTRODUCTION

After the Treaty of Tilsit in 1807, Prussia was relegated to the second rank of European powers. Of the army which had been 235,000 men strong at the outbreak of war, only 63,000 were left. Most of its fortresses with their military stores had been handed over to the French, many of them without resistance. Prussia had lost half its territory and high reparations restricted the financial flexibility of the state for years. The Prussian king laid the foundations for rectifying the situation through far-reaching reform of the Prussian state and the modernisation of its army, whose tactics were greatly improved and whose incompetent leaders were replaced. Great emphasis was laid on training the soldiers and officers for all the situations they could encounter in war. The recruitment of mercenaries from the lower levels of society was stopped and corporal punishment all but abolished.

As a result, the public image of the common soldier was significantly enhanced. This was one of the preconditions for the introduction of general conscription in Prussia – in 1813 for the duration of the war, in 1814 for times of peace too – which increased the potential strength of the army radically.

Through the victories of its army, formed from patriotic citizens and led by capable officers and generals, the Prussian state re-emerged as an important player in the field of European politics. Numerically, the main part of the army was the infantry: the regular infantry, who formed the backbone of this, are the subject of this book.

Friedrich Wilhelm III, King of Prussia, in a general's uniform, painted in Paris by Gerard in 1814. He was born in 1770, succeeded his father to the throne in 1797 and died in 1840. Every year his birthday, 3 August, was celebrated with parades and festivities by the whole army. He was beloved by his soldiers, and his boldness and courage in battle only increased this.

# CHRONOLOGY

**9 July 1807** Treaty of Tilsit establishes peace between Prussia and France. The former loses half its territory and has to pay extremely high reparations.

**25 July 1807** The committee for military reorganisation is installed, presided over by General-Major von Scharnhorst. This committee will be at the heart of the Prussian army reforms.

**3 August 1808** New Articles of War are created, which regulate the duties and punishment of the soldiers. Corporal punishment is all but abolished.

**8 September 1808** Convention of Paris. Dictated by Napoleon, the strength of the Prussian army is to be reduced to a maximum of 42,000 men, including 10 line regiments comprising 22,000 men.

**27 March 1809** Instructions on the use of the 3rd rank for skirmishing are published.

**16 July 1809** Instructions on the use of infantry are published.

**14 May 1811** Formation of the Normal-Infanterie-Bataillon, whose purpose is to standardise drill and service of all the infantry units within the Prussian army. It is stationed in Berlin and composed of officers and men taken from all line regiments for the duration of one year, after which period they are to return to their regiments and be replaced by others.

**15 January 1812** New Prussian regulations for exercise are published.

**24 February 1812** Alliance between Prussia and France. Prussia has to provide an Auxiliary Corps of 20,000 men against Russia.

**30 December 1812** Convention of Tauroggen. General-Lieutenant von Yorck declares the neutrality of the Prussian Auxiliary Corps under his command and signs an armistice with the Russian General-Major von Diebitsch.

**1 February 1813** Each line battalion of the army is ordered to form a reserve battalion, providing NCOs and experienced men for its cadre.

**28 February 1813** Treaty of Kalisch, an alliance between Prussia and Russia.

**16 March 1813** Declaration of war against France.

**5 June 1813** Armistice of Poischwitz between France and the Allies.

**1 July 1813** Creation of a 12th line regiment and 12 Reserve-Infanterie-Regimenter from battalions newly raised in early 1813.

**16 August 1813** Reopening of hostilities. Austria joins the Allies.

**16 to 19 October 1813** 'Battle of the Nations' at Leipzig. Napoleon is defeated and retreats into France.

**1 January 1814** The Allies cross the River Rhine and invade France from several locations.

**31 March 1814** Occupation of Paris by the Allies.

**30 May 1814** First Treaty of Paris, and the return of Louis XVIII to the throne of France.

**30 October 1814** Official start of the Congress of Vienna.

**7 and 25 March 1815** Reorganisation of the line infantry into 32 regiments.

**25 March 1815** Military Alliance of Prussia, Russia, Austria and Great Britain against Napoleon, who has returned from exile.

**9 June 1815** Treaty of Vienna, which settles the political order of Europe for the coming decades.

**18 June 1815** Battle of Belle-Alliance (Waterloo). Complete defeat of Napoleon's army.

**7 July 1815** Second occupation of Paris.

**20 November 1815** Second Treaty of Paris. France has to pay high reparations to Prussia.

# BECOMING A PRUSSIAN SOLDIER

On 17 December 1807, an *AKO* (*Allerhöchste Kabinetts-Order*, a decree issued by the Royal Cabinet) put an end to the active recruitment of *Ausländer* (foreigners) in large numbers. This meant that there were now only two ways that a man could enter Prussian military service – conscription, or voluntary enlistment without bounty.

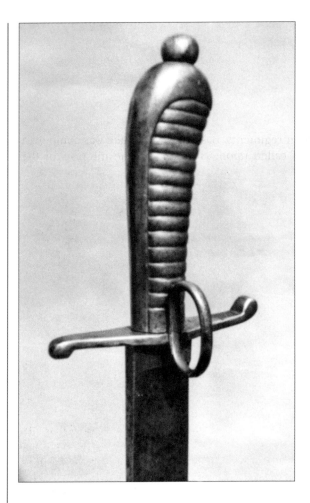

ABOVE  **Brass hilt, 137mm high, of the *Füsilier* sword *M1787*. Sabres of this type that were produced later did not have the finger ring, sometimes it was even filed off on the older swords. The blade is 483mm long, 39mm wide at the hilt and at its shoulder 33.2mm wide. (Armeemuseum Friedrich der Große Plassenburg, Collection Windsheimer)**

ABOVE RIGHT  **Details of the clasp and the markings on the upper part of a Prussian scabbard. Scabbards were of brown leather before 1816, only after that date were they blackened. Sometimes the leather covered a wooden scabbard, which proved useful as an additional protection against rust. This item is marked with the rank and name of the company's commander. In 1806, von Strenge was Major in the *Infanterie-Regiment Schimonsky* (No. 40). (Armeemuseum Friedrich der Große Plassenburg, Collection Windsheimer)**

RIGHT  **Detail of the workmanship on the rear of this scabbard. The brass collar at the bottom is covered by the leather so that only its tip remains visible.**

## Conscription

Conscription was regulated by the *Kantonreglement* of 12 February 1792, issued by Friedrich Wilhelm II. In its introduction the king laid out the obligation of the government to defend the country against its enemies and to ensure the security of the possessions of his subjects, as well as the obligation for all his subjects to serve militarily.

The country was divided into *Kantone* (recruiting cantons), which were assigned to certain regiments. Basically, every male was compelled to become a soldier if called upon. However, 'in the interests of the welfare of the state' there were more than a few exceptions made.

Firstly, some regions and cities inherited the privilege of full exemption from conscription. This exemption had been granted to them by the Prussian Electors, long before the position of the Prussian kings became absolute in the 18th century. In 1808 the towns of Berlin, Potsdam, Brandenburg and Breslau were the only remaining parts of the kingdom still to enjoy this privilege.

In the other areas, in which the *Kantonreglement* was in force, two types of men could avoid conscription: those whose financial or social condition allowed it and those exempt provided that certain conditions were met.

Those unconditionally exempt were as follows:
1 the nobility
2 commoners who owned estates with a value greater than 12,000 *Reichstaler*
3 civil servants
4 the sons of university professors
5 those with a personal fortune of more than 10,000 *Reichstaler* (as long as they were not craftsmen or peasants) and their sons.

Foreigners who had settled in Prussia were exempt as well, together with their sons and any servants they had brought with them. If they built a house or cultivated designated wasteland, their sons (provided they were born in Prussia) were also exempt.

Those who were exempt provided that certain conditions were met were as follows:
1 those studying
2 those who were active on their own account in commerce or agriculture.

The exact conditions were laid out in paragraph 14 of the *Kantonreglement*: 'if [these types of exempt men] begin to lead a roaming or an unstable lifestyle or leave their chosen occupation, they shall once more become liable for military service.' From 24 May 1793 students had to demonstrate that they were engaged in study, as there were numerous abuses of this exemption.

The *AKO* of 21 November 1808 assigned the cantons to the regiments of the new army. It did not alter the rules for exemption, as there were no difficulties in finding sufficient recruitment for the army (which was limited to a maximum of 42,000 men). The men preferred for recruits were those 'most appropriate for serving their country', e.g. soldiers from dissolved regiments that had returned to their cantons (especially those who had served less than 10 years and were still young and fit for service). The sons of soldiers were preferred as recruits, too. Men with bad health or 'acknowledged bad conduct' were not to be recruited.

Those men not yet selected as recruits still remained liable for military service until they passed the age of 25, thus forming a kind of regimental recruiting reserve. They were named *Kantonisten*.

From 6 June 1809, the sons of former *Ausländer* (a foreigner not subject to the Prussian state) soldiers living in Prussia were to be regarded as natives of the country and fully liable for military service. After 8 September 1809 the sons of any soldiers born in Berlin, Potsdam, Brandenburg or Breslau lost the rights of exemption granted to their residents.

The *AKO* of 9 February 1813 suspended all the above-mentioned exemptions 'for the duration of the war'. Those who were previously exempt and were aged between 17 and 24 retained the right to enter the military voluntarily and choose their unit themselves, preferably in one of the detachments of *Freiwillige Jäger* (volunteer riflemen). All the others could be selected as recruits for the field army or, if they were between 25 and 40, for the *Landwehr*.

This *AKO* did provide for certain exemptions, as follows:

1  all 'weak' young men between the ages of 17 and 24
2  the heads of households whose fathers were dead
3  the eldest sons of widows
4  the single bread-winner of families who, without him, would be helpless
5  civil servants and the clergy.

Following the cessation of hostilities with France in 1814 an *AKO* of 27 May cancelled all the suspensions introduced by the *AKO* of 9 February this year. However, on 3 September 1814, the *Gesetz über die Verpflichtung zum Kriegsdienste* (law on the obligation to perform military service) was signed by the king. Every man born within the Prussian state and above the age of 20 was compelled to defend his country. There were no exemptions any more. Military service lasted three years in the standing army with another two years on stand-by, thus forming a reserve for the army in case of war.

## The Krümper system

The main aim of the Prussian army reforms was to lay the foundations for the re-establishment of Prussian military power. One of the prerequisites for this was to create a reserve which would permit a swift and efficient expansion of the army in times of war.

In order to comply with the restriction of the army to 42,000 men, an *AKO* of 6 August 1808 ordered each company to call up some five recruits per month. In exchange, five experienced men were dismissed, so that the effective strength under arms did not change.

These experienced men were called '*Krümper*', a word with a complicated etymology which literally means 'shrinkers': early thought had been that in times of war they would replace losses and as such prevent the units' strength from shrinking. After their period of service they returned to their home villages or towns and did not receive any more pay, but they could be recalled to arms at any time, forming a kind of regimental reserve. Former soldiers who had been in the army before 1807 and were living in the canton were also classified as *Krümper*, as long as they were still fit for military service.

The number of *Krümper* and the duration of their stay in the companies varied from unit to unit. For transforming a recruit into a good soldier, 3 months of training were thought necessary, but, as an officer in the *1. Schlesisches Infanterie-Regiment* pointed out with regard to the *Krümper* of 1810/11: 'it seemed to be important only to give these men an idea of the soldier's life, because no great detail was deemed necessary for the war.'

The reserve battalions raised via the *Krümper* system at the end of 1812 and beginning of 1813 had still to undergo significant training before they were ready for field service. However, without the *Krümper* system this task would have been much more difficult.

## Selecting recruits

In each district, lists of all the eligible males were to be kept by the *Landrat* (district magistrate). These were updated once a year in co-operation with the priests of the parishes, who kept track of deaths and births.

Once a year the commander of each of the six brigades (administrative formations in use in times of peace before 1813) gave the number of recruits his brigade needed to the chamber of the provinces in which his brigade was stationed. The chambers distributed these numbers to the districts, according to the number of inhabitants, and the district magistrate distributed their share to the parishes.

On a given date, all young men between 20 and 25 who were liable for military service had to gather in the capital of the district. Only those fit for military service were desired, so all conscripts were examined by a surgeon and an officer. From those found fit the recruits were selected, sometimes lots were drawn for this purpose. Their military service would last 20 years.

To match the much higher numbers of recruits required in spring 1813, men who were not in full health were also accepted. On 22 March 1813 *General-Stabs-Chirurgus der Armee* Dr Görcke, the head of the Prussian medical service, issued a detailed instruction on how to select men for military service. The conscripts had to be inspected – whenever possible – by military surgeons and assigned to one of five classes:

1 Every 'healthy, well-formed and fit man who possesses good sight, hearing and teeth and who is able to perform certain common movements with his body' was considered fit for any military field service, be it in the infantry, cavalry, artillery, or train. Minor faults such as varicose veins or curved fingers were passed.

2 Those soldiers who were unable to do longer marches due to bad feet or legs, but had no other defects, were considered still fit for military field service in the cavalry.

3 The following were considered only fit for 'military duties in garrison': men who had served in the military for a long while, but whose limbs had developed 'a certain bluntness'; those with bad (but not very bad) sight; men with painful feet; men with swollen or painful throats; men who were short of breath; men with deformed but functioning limbs;

Karl August von Stutterheim commanding a battalion of the *2. Westpreußisches Infanterie-Regiment*, probably between 1810 and 1812. The epaulets with lace around indicate the rank of a staff officer (Major and above). Born on 20 November 1759 and starting his military carreer in the infantry on 1 March 1773, von Stutterheim was transferred to the *Infanterie-Regiment von Courbière* (No. 58) in 1797. He stayed in this regiment when it changed its name to *2. Westpreußisches* in 1808 and was promoted to Major in 1803 and *Oberst-Lieutenant* in February 1812. In May 1813 von Stutterheim was transferred to the Silesian Landwehr, in July 1813 he became commander of the 11. *Reserve-Infanterie-Regiment*. He attained the rank of General Major in 1814 and died an accidental death in 1820.

men with one leg shorter than the other; men with no front teeth but who could still bite open a cartridge; men with minor hernias; and men with missing fingers, as long as they had their thumbs.

4 Those men who were ill but who would be expected to recover, and young men aged between 17 and 20 who were 'not yet fully formed' were considered temporarily unfit for military service.

5 Men who suffered from serious illnesses, physical defects or disfigurements were considered 'Forever unfit for Royal military service'.

Because so many men had to be examined at the beginning of 1813, examinations could not have been very thorough. Each man had to undress only if he claimed to possess hidden defects which would make him unfit for military service.

Naturally, there were men who tried to beat the system. Johann Karl Hechel, aged 23, a stableman from Mahlenziehn in the province of Brandenburg, was called to be examined on 1 March 1813 in the town of Genthin, 20km distant:

'My master didn't want to lose me and believed that I would also be happy to stay put. He rubbed snuff in my eyes to make them look sore so that on examination I should be declared unfit for soldiering.'

But Hechel was more patriotic than his master expected him to be. On his way to Genthin he washed his eyes in the nearby River Buckau and became a soldier, leaving us a very vivid account of his military service from 1813 to 1815.

### The soldier's height

The minimum height requirement to be a Prussian soldier was 5 *Fuß* (1.57m). The 1811 survey of the *Kantonisten* of the line regiments gives the average height of the Prussian soldier as 1.63m. In fact, for the 11 line regiments in existence at that time the average height may have been slightly higher, if we assume that men of greater height would have been preferred for military service: the shorter ones would have been used as the reserve in the regimental canton.

As a general rule, taller men who were not transferred to the guards entered the grenadier companies of the regiment. The most agile and

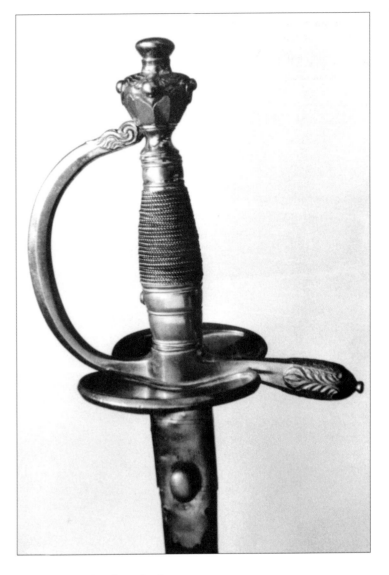

An officers' sword. This variation first appeared in 1805 and was used until the 1830s. The hilt is 165mm high, of gilded brass, and the grip is wound round with silver thread. The Solingen blade, with flower and trophy etchings, is 857mm long and 25mm wide at the hilt. (Armeemuseum Friedrich der Große Plassenburg, Collection Windsheimer)

'Old Prussian' sabre M 1715 with 'old Prussian' tassel. Although new colours were prescribed for the sword tassels in 1808, their shape did not change. (Wehrgeschichtliches Museum Rastatt)

quick-witted should have been assigned to the *Füsilier* battalion: usually, though, the shortest men were selected for this unit. As an officer in the *Füsilier* battalion of the *1. Schlesisches Infanterie-Regiment*, von Blumen, remarked, 'The later *Füsiliere* were only distinguished by their short stature and their black leather belts.'

In 1810 the minimum height for individuals entering the guards was '7 *Zoll*' (i.e. 5 *Fuß* 7 *Zoll* = 1.75m), but this height is found only in the first two battalions of the *Garde-Regiment zu Fuß*.

When the *Garde-Füsilier-Bataillon* was formed in 1809, the men selected for it from the army were to have a height of between 1.66m and 1.73m. The *2. Garde-Regiment zu Fuß* was established in summer 1813 from the existing line battalions, so that the men's height represented the average found in an ordinary line regiment.

## Distributing the men to the units

The *AKO* of 8 July 1809 severed the link between the regiments and their respective cantons. The commanders of the six administrative brigades received the right to distribute recruits to the regiments 'in accordance with their qualifications for the different arms'. For the infantry, which didn't require any special qualification, things changed little.

The recruits had to gather at a given date 'in a suitable place' in order to be selected for line infantry, light infantry, cavalry or artillery by a commission of officers from all arms. Within each arm, the men could be distributed to the regiments by lot or by the decision of the brigade or regimental commanders, if these were present. If individuals volunteered for certain companies or units, their wishes were to be given preference if possible.

In spring 1813, before Prussia declared its alliance with Russia, the recruits were gathered in areas that were not occupied by the French. Johann Hechel had to march with 610 other recruits from the province of Brandenburg to the town of Liegnitz in Silesia:

'Here our patriotic pride would be put to the test. From 10 o'clock in the morning until the same hour at night we had to stand in formation at the roadside, awaiting selection for the different arms. But we did not complain.'

The length of time, 12 hours for 600 men, indicates that each man was questioned prior to the decision as to which arm he should join. Hechel was chosen for one of the infantry reserve battalions. In the summer of 1813, his battalion was dissolved and he was transferred to the *Füsilier* battalion of the *2. Brandenburgisches Infanterie-Regiment.*

## Voluntary enlistment

Military service was attractive to men without means and economic prospects, as the army provided the basics of life: food, accommodation and clothing.

This was the reason why Friedrich Wilhelm Beeger, a fatherless son whose mother and other relations did not care too much for him, entered service. He became an apprentice to a hunter, but after one year his clothing was in 'the saddest condition'. His master provided him with

A Prussian officer's sash. Made from silver thread with two stripes of black silk, it had to be long enough to be wound round the body twice. (Blüchermuseum Kaub)

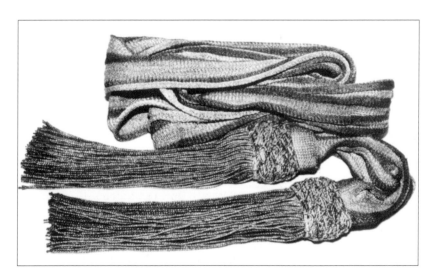

food, but did give him a salary. He could see no way of buying new clothes for himself, and finally decided to walk to Berlin to become a soldier. There, at the age of 17, Beeger joined the *Infanterie-Regiment von Arnim* (No. 13) in 1799 or 1800.

In 1806 he was taken prisoner when his battalion defended Lübeck against the French. He tried to escape from captivity twice, but was finally forced to join the Westphalian army, in which he rose to the rank of lieutenant. Sent to Spain with his regiment, in 1810 he deserted and after spending some time with a group of Spanish guerrillas, he volunteered to serve in the British *King's German Legion* and was sent back to England to its depot. There he changed his mind and, driven by a strong sense of patriotism, he decided to return to Prussia, crossing the Channel in a smuggling boat.

Through a letter of recommendation, which he had received in England, he was introduced to a Prussian general in Berlin and finally succeeded in being allowed to join the *Leib-Infanterie-Regiment*, but only at the rank of an *Unteroffizier* and with the pay of a simple soldier. But he was content.

After 1807, *Ausländer* were still admitted as volunteers, but they had to be Germans, of good conduct (no deserters were allowed), fit for service and not older than 30 years. Preferably they should come from the Prussian provinces lost in the war of 1806/7. They were engaged for at least three years and did not receive financial reward. Foreign recruitment did not play any important part in the Prussian army after 1808.

Sometimes, on campaign, even prisoners could become Prussian soldiers. On 2 January 1814, near Saarlouis, *Füsilier* Hechel, of the *2. Brandenburgisches Infanterie-Regiment* took a French soldier prisoner:

'Quickly I took his musket and made him prisoner. Now, he spoke German and I came to learn that he was Swiss. So I left him all his belongings, and was happy to do so when he said that he wanted to enter service with us. He immediately joined our 11th company, but when we came close to the Swiss border, he deserted.'

## Women soldiers

A volunteer of a very rare kind was a girl, Sophia Dorothea Friederike Krüger, born in October 1789 in Friedland in Mecklenburg-Strelitz. At the end of 1812 she had been sent by her father to Anklam in (Prussian) Pomerania to become a tailor. She used what she learned to make male clothing for herself, cut off her hair and volunteered in March 1813, entering the 1st Company of the reserve battalion of the *Kolbergsches Infanterie-Regiment*. In August 1813, when this regiment's 1st Battalion was transferred to the newly formed *2. Garde-Regiment zu Fuß*, her reserve battalion became the new 1st Battalion.

She soon gained the respect of her comrades by her outstanding bravery and presence of mind, always volunteering for dangerous tasks. Her gender was probably a 'public secret' within her company. It seems in one early incident she betrayed herself during an attack, shouting out with a high-pitched, feminine voice. When she was found out she was allowed to stay in the ranks thanks only to the protection of the commander of her brigade, *General-Lieutenant* von Borstell: she promised him to be brave and remain chaste, which she did.

During the Battle of Dennewitz on 6 September 1813, she was made *Unteroffizier*. Later she also received the Iron Cross 2nd class and the Russian order of St. George 5th class for refusing to leave the battlefield despite having being wounded in the shoulder and foot. Afterwards, in a hospital in Berlin, her gender became publicly known. As her moral behaviour was proven to be above doubt, she still was allowed to stay in the army. She returned to her regiment in time to take part in the 1814 and 1815 campaigns too.

A fellow-countryman of hers reported an incident in 1816, when he visited her in Berlin. Whilst drinking with her in an inn, she was asked for help by a few soldiers of a Pomeranian regiment, who had been insulted and pushed out of the dancing hall in the same place by some soldiers of the Royal Guards.

'She immediately got up and went there. I followed and was witness to her thundering at these tall guardsmen with her female voice, blaming them for their foolish haughtiness and their uncomrade-like behaviour, reminding them that the Pomeranians had bled, suffered and done infinitely more than the Guards, and setting them right in such a manner, that they didn't know how to answer and got on well with their brothers in arms from that day onward.'

In 1816 she was allowed on her request to leave the service and the Prussian king granted her a yearly pension of 50 *Reichstaler* (her annual pay as an active *Unteroffizier* had been 54 *Reichstaler*). When she married shortly afterwards, and on the birth of her first child, she received presents from the Prussian king too.

Auguste Krüger, as she was generally known despite her christian name, died in May 1848. She was the only woman in the Prussian army that was allowed to remain in service after her gender was discovered. There were also another dozen or so women documented who served, all of whom had to hide their real identity. The women serving as Prussian soldiers will not be much higher.

# CONDITIONS OF SERVICE

### The composition of an infantry regiment

Each Prussian infantry regiment consisted of two *Musketier* and one *Füsilier* battalion of four companies each. In addition, there were two *Grenadier* companies. The *Garde-Regiment zu Fuß* did not have any grenadiers, but *the Leib-Infanterie-Regiment* had one complete *Grenadier* battalion of four companies instead, named *Leib-Grenadier-Bataillon*. The denomination '*Füsilier-Bataillon*' replaced the name '*Leichtes Bataillon*' (light battalion) following an *AKO* of 1 December 1809.

The *Musketier* companies in each regiment were numbered from 1 to 8. The *Füsilier* companies were numbered separately from 1 to 4: in 1815, they received the numbers 9 to 12 instead.

The *Grenadier* companies of the two regiments from a province were permanently grouped together in one battalion under a single commander. The six battalions of the Prussian army were named *I. Ostpreußisches Grenadier-Bataillon* (from the 1st and 2nd East Prussian regiments), *Pommersches Grenadier-Bataillon*, *II. Ostpreußisches Grenadier-*

*Bataillon* (from the 3rd and 4th East Prussian regiments), *Westpreußisches Grenadier-Bataillon*, *Leib-Grenadier-Bataillon* and *Schlesisches Grenadier-Bataillon*.

On 14 and 19 October 1814 the six *Grenadier* battalions were separated from their regiments and formed into two independent grenadier regiments. The Russian Tsar and the Austrian Emperor were invited to be the *Regiments-Chefs* of these regiments and the new units became *Grenadier-Regiment Kaiser Alexander* and *Grenadier-Regiment Kaiser Franz*.

In early 1813, 52 new reserve and depot battalions were formed and were (at least technically) attached to the existing 12 regiments. These battalions changed their designation several times, and tracing their development is beyond the scope of this book.

Each regiment had a garrison company too, which was filled with those soldiers who were no longer fit for field service.

## The soldier's pay

Pay had to be distributed to each soldier in front of the whole company and in the presence of an officer on the 1st, 11th and 21st of each month. If the soldier was absent on leave for 10 days or more, he would not get his pay. The money thus saved remained the property of the government.

This pay seems to have been relatively low. In the 'old army' (pre-1807) the pay of the private soldier was 2 *Reichstaler* (i.e. 48 *Groschen*) per month, but was distributed every five days. Wilhelm Beeger recalls these times:

Monthly pay in times of peace for the infantry, as ordered on 19th May 1809. For easier comparison, the salary of all ranks has been converted into *Groschen* in an extra column. The battalion quartermaster in the line infantry had an increase of 10 *Reichstaler* (240 *Groschen*) per month. The commander of a grenadier battalion received 3 *Rationen*.

| Rank | Guards Reichstaler | Guards Groschen | Guards = Groschen | Line infantry Reichstaler | Line infantry Groschen | Line infantry = Groschen | Garrison company Reichstaler | Garrison company Groschen | Garrison company = Groschen | All Portionen (a horse's daily ration) | All Rationen (a man's daily ration) |
|---|---|---|---|---|---|---|---|---|---|---|---|
| Regimental commander | 216 | 16 | 5200 | 208 | 8 | 5000 | | | | | 4 |
| Staff officer | 158 | 8 | 3800 | 150 | | 3600 | 66 | 16 | 1600 | | 2 |
| Capitain | 108 | 8 | 2600 | 100 | | 2400 | 50 | | 1200 | | |
| Stabs-Capitain | 40 | | 960 | 30 | | 720 | 25 | | 600 | | |
| Premier-Lieutenant | 30 | | 720 | 25 | | 600 | 25 | | 600 | | |
| Adjutant | 26 | | 624 | 23 | | 552 | | | | | 1 |
| Regimental quartermaster | 33 | | 792 | 30 | | 720 | | | | | 1 |
| Seconde-Lieutenant | 20 | | 480 | 17 | | 408 | 17 | | 408 | | |
| Feldwebel | 10 | 16 | 256 | 6 | 12 | 156 | 6 | 12 | 156 | 1 | |
| Portepeefähnrich | 6 | | 144 | 6 | | 144 | | | | 1 | |
| Sergeant/Regiments-Tambour | 5 | 20 | 140 | 4 | 12 | 108 | 4 | 12 | 108 | 1 | |
| Corporal/Bataillons-Tambour | 4 | 12 | 108 | 3 | 12 | 84 | 3 | 12 | 84 | 1 | |
| Hautboist | 5 | | 120 | 4 | | 96 | | | | 1 | |
| Gefreiter | 3 | 5.5 | 77.5 | 2 | 2.75 | 50.75 | | | | 1 | |
| Gemeiner/Tambour/Hornist | 3 | 3 | 75 | 2 | | 48 | 2 | | 48 | 1 | |
| | | | | | | | | | | | |
| Regimental surgeon | 50 | | 1200 | 40 | | 960 | | | | | |
| Battalion surgeon | | | | 20 | | 480 | | | | 1 | |
| Company surgeon | 15 | 12 | 372 | 10 | | 240 | 19 | | 456 | 1 | |
| Gun smith | 6 | | 144 | 5 | | 120 | | | | | |
| Gun stocker | 6 | | 144 | 5 | | 120 | | | | | |

| | Height in feet | Height in metres (m) | 1. Ostpreußisches Infanterie-Regiment | 2. Ostpreußisches Infanterie-Regiment | 3. Ostpreußisches Infanterie-Regiment | 4. Ostpreußisches Infanterie-Regiment | 1. Pommersches Infanterie-Regiment | Colbergsches Infanterie-Regiment | Leib Infanterie-Regiment | 1. Westpreußisches Infanterie-Regiment | 2. Westpreußisches Infanterie-Regiment | 1. Schlesisches Infanterie-Regiment | 2. Schlesisches Infanterie-Regiment | Total |
|---|---|---|---|---|---|---|---|---|---|---|---|---|---|---|
| Number of households in the regiment's cantons | | | 14195 | 14667 | 43186 | 28081 | 38717 | 37800 | 43677 | 35303 | 35505 | 57651 | 43012 | **391794** |
| Number of unexempted recruits in the canton with a height of | 5 Fuß | 1.57m | 622 | 903 | 1576 | 1709 | unknown | 2543 | 3170 | 990 | 2989 | 1785 | 1121 | **17408** |
| | 5 Fuß 1 Zoll | 1.59m | 1434 | 1412 | 3497 | 3182 | 2218 | 1210 | 3908 | 1704 | 1502 | 2860 | 2129 | **25056** |
| | 5 Fuß 2 Zoll | 1.62m | 1884 | 1083 | 4683 | 3431 | 2285 | 1774 | 3698 | 1952 | 2040 | 3423 | 2624 | **28877** |
| | 5 Fuß 3 Zoll | 1.65m | 1172 | 651 | 4669 | 2559 | 2373 | 1510 | 2987 | 1572 | 1437 | 2977 | 2154 | **24061** |
| | 5 Fuß 4 Zoll | 1.67m | 703 | 247 | 3076 | 1358 | 1720 | 768 | 1454 | 878 | 579 | 2079 | 1061 | **13923** |
| | 5 Fuß 5 Zoll | 1.70m | 299 | 93 | 1274 | 491 | 846 | 264 | 638 | 325 | 131 | 1017 | 484 | **5862** |
| | 5 Fuß 6 Zoll | 1.73m | 108 | 28 | 391 | 150 | 364 | 110 | 282 | 107 | 35 | 418 | 206 | **2199** |
| | 5 Fuß 7 Zoll | 1.75m | 28 | 12 | 82 | 47 | 162 | 44 | 105 | 31 | 5 | 162 | 80 | **758** |
| | 5 Fuß 8 Zoll | 1.77m | 8 | 6 | 37 | 8 | 48 | 17 | 44 | 14 | 2 | 44 | 17 | **245** |
| | 5 Fuß 9 Zoll | 1.80m | 1 | | 6 | 10 | 11 | 7 | 15 | 1 | 1 | 24 | 3 | **79** |
| | 5 Fuß 10 Zoll | 1.83m | 2 | | 1 | | 6 | 2 | | 2 | | 4 | 2 | **19** |
| | 5 Fuß 11 Zoll | 1.86m | | | | | 1 | | | | | 4 | | **5** |
| **Total** | | | **6261** | **4435** | **19292** | **12945** | **10034** | **8249** | **16301** | **7576** | **8721** | **14797** | **9881** | **118492** |
| Single sons and heirs | | | 270 | 210 | 647 | 2335 | 586 | 10386 | 447 | 1115 | 1297 | 1593 | 509 | **19395** |
| **Total of the two first categories** | | | **6531** | **4645** | **19939** | **15280** | **10620** | **18635** | **16748** | **8691** | **10018** | **16390** | **10390** | **137887** |
| Men below 5 Fuß (1.57m) | | | 2237 | 2881 | 5624 | 4156 | 10936 | 3590 | 0 | 5690 | 15338 | 10468 | 5027 | **65947** |
| **Total of all three categories (= the strength of the canton)** | | | **8768** | **7526** | **25563** | **19436** | **21556** | **22225** | **16748** | **14381** | **25356** | **26858** | **15417** | **203834** |

**Overview of the potential number of recruits of the 11 Prussian line regiments in 1811. The table lists only men between 18 and 40 years and does not contain the class of men who were exempted without condition. This statistic is based on the reports of the regiments, who did not always follow an identical system of classification. The Colbersches Infanterie-Regiment listed those men who could not be drafted immediately (for example because they were ill or just 18 years old and not yet strong enough for the military) in the category of 'Single heirs and sons'. And it is hard to believe that there were no men below 5 Fuß (1.57m) in the canton of the Leib-Infanterie-Regiment. The average size of the unexempted recruits was 1.63m.**

'After deducting the expenses for cleaning and other living costs, the 8 *Groschen* pay received every 5 days did not suffice to satisfy the needs of the soldier even with great thrift.'

When Beeger rejoined the *Leib-Infanterie-Regiment* in 1811, as an additional *Unteroffizier*, he received only a private's pay. He could preserve 'a smartness better than that of my comrades' only by using his own savings. As the prices in Berlin, where his regiment was garrisoned, were particularly high, we can assume that regiments stationed in the provinces would have been better off.

## Company funds

The companies had several funds supplied by the government whose administration followed basic regulations dated 11 July 1808.

The first fund was that of the *Gewehrgelder* (musket money). One *Groschen* per man every month was paid in, based on the regulation strength of the company. The fund was intended for the repair of the company's muskets. Money that was not spent during the month could be carried over to the next month, but it was not to be used for any other purpose.

The second fund was that of the *Kompanie-Unkosten* (company expenses). It was allocated at 2 *Groschen* per man for the line infantry, 2 *Groschen* 3 *Pfennig* per man for the guard infantry and 2 *Groschen* 6 *Pfennig* *per man* for the garrison companies. This sum was also paid monthly and based on the regulation strength of the company. This fund was used for repairing uniforms, feeding the sick, supporting the infirmaries, paying the funeral expenses of soldiers and the purchase and maintenance of musical instruments.

Both funds were administered by the officer directly below the company commander, assisted by the company's *Feldwebel* and *Kapitain d'armes*. They had to provide accounts to the company commander each month. Once a year these monthly company accounts were audited by a regimental commission consisting of a staff officer, a *Kapitain*, a *Lieutenant* and the regimental quartermaster.

Any surplus of the *Kompanie-Unkosten* was administered by this regimental commission and was only to be spent 'for the good of the common soldier, for his military education or training'. Extraordinary regimental expenses could be paid from this surplus too, after having been approved by the king himself. 'Any expenses for irregular decoration or musicians above the strength allowed by regulation' were strictly forbidden: in 1814 and 1815, in many regiments the officers made private collections in order to improve the standards of regimental music.

For the *Medizingelder* fund (medicine money), 2 *Groschen* were allocated per month for every man present under arms. This fund was administered by the regimental or battalion surgeon.

The *Kleine Montierungsgelder* (money for minor uniform parts) was paid to the regiment for purchasing small items, so that advantage could be taken of local suppliers and transport costs saved. For NCOs and musicians, the rate was 21 *Groschen* in the guard infantry and 16 *Groschen* 6 *Pfennig* in the line infantry. For ordinary soldiers the rate was 17 *Groschen*, and for drummers and buglers the rate was 12 *Groschen* 8 *Pfennig*. This fund was administered and the materials purchased by a regimental commission consisting of the regimental quartermaster and one officer of each rank from staff officer down to *Seconde-Lieutenant*. Two NCOs had to keep the lists. In a detached battalion, this commission consisted only of the battalion's quartermaster or a *Feldwebel*, one company commander, one *Premier-* and *Seconde-Lieutenant* each and two NCOs. The soldiers' wives were to be engaged 'as much as possible' in making and supplying such items: this aspect was organised by the commission too. The members of this commission were elected by all the officers of their respective ranks. Half of them – except the quartermaster – were to be replaced each year.

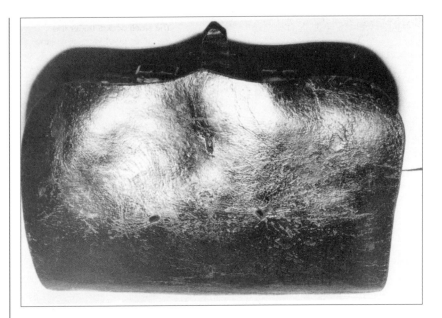

Prussian cartridge pouch M 1809. The outer dimensions of the box were 22cm by 13.5cm by 7cm. The three holes in the front flap were used for attaching the oval brass plate for Musketiere and Grenadiere, which had small metal loops soldered to its back. The cartridge pouch could be fixed to a leather button on the sabre belt by the horizontal white leather strap. (Collection Freyda)

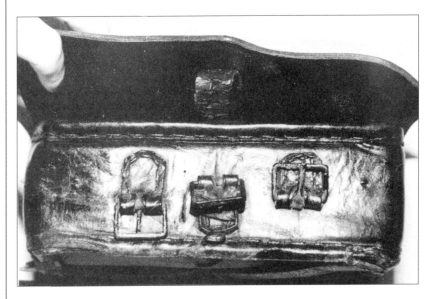

The bottom of the cartridge pouch. The belt to carry it was fixed with blackened iron buckles, measuring 2cm by 3cm, the front flap was secured by an identical buckle. Typical for the Prussian cartridge pouches from the Seven Years War until after the Napoleonic Wars was that the side parts and the bottom were made of one single piece of leather. The French and British cartridge pouches of the Napoleonic Wars, on the contrary, had the front, bottom and rear made out of a single piece of leather.

For *Kleine Ausgaben* (small expenses) there was a monthly allowance of 5 *Reichstaler*, which was paid to each company commander. He did not have to keep account of this fund, but from this sum had to provide for all writing materials, his share of the salary of the regimental scribe and any administrative postal expenses.

## Living quarters

A provisional regulation of 24 December 1808, followed by the *AKO* of 17 March 1810, regulated all aspects of quartering officers and men.

The soldiers were generally quartered in houses in the town, and the distribution was organised by the town councils. The hosts received financial compensation from the government for all their expenses, which amounted to 1 *Reichstaler* in average towns and 1 *Reichstaler*

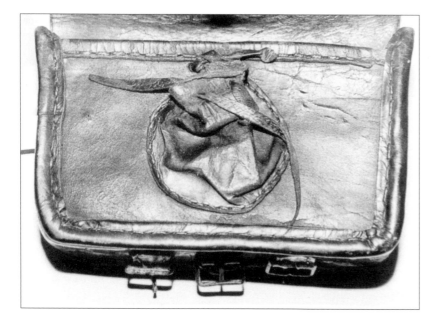

The small pocket under the front flap, used for storing extra flintstones and a worm for pulling out unfired cartridges. Its diameter is 8cm. Inside, the cartridge pouch is strengthened by a box made from iron sheeting and divided into two compartments. The box's dimensions were 200mm by 55mm by 55mm.

Rear view of the same cartridge pouch. The diagonal leather strap has been added at a later date.

8 *Groschen* in more expensive towns. Each company had to be quartered as close together as possible.

*Feldwebel* were entitled to a single room, but privates and *Unteroffiziere* were quartered in rooms averaging four men each. The rooms had to be 'in a healthy part of the house' and accessible by 'ordinary stairs'. Each room had to contain one table, one stool per man, hangers for the uniforms and one sleeping place per man, complete with mattress, straw, pillow and blanket. No more than two men should sleep in one bed: sharing a bed was not unusual, as this also happened in civilian life.

In winter, the soldiers had the right to make use of a heated room during the day, and lighting until 9 p.m. (tallow candles or oil lamps were a cost factor too). For cooking, they were allowed to use the host's kitchen and had to be provided with the cooking equipment they needed.

# TRAINING

In addition to basic training, great importance was given to the training of skirmishers. The third rank of all companies was used for skirmishing. In the *Füsilier* battalions, all three ranks were used for this purpose. Field service was practised every year in autumn manoeuvres.

After the wars, Max von Busse, an officer in the *11. Reserve-Infanterie-Regiment*, summed up his experiences of training recruits in wartime as follows:

> The recruits will receive their muskets on the first day of training, ready to start immediately with the first movements of charging arms. These will be continued in the following days, and, being the main focus of exercise, will be continued daily, so that after 14 days they can move on to firing, first with blanks, and then at a practice target. Instruction in other movements will have but little time devoted, and should be left completely until the men are sure in the movements of charging their arms. Instruction in skirmishing, including the signals, and the details of daily service will also start on the first day, to be followed within the first eight days by instruction in field service. Training in marching, including the movements, is to be used only for variety and should not have much time invested in it; the time spent on their way to the army shall be used for this instruction.
>
> When the recruits, who have been trained in such a hasty manner, are integrated into the rank and file, they should be placed in the middle files of the *Sektionen*, regardless of their height, and the flank files of the *Sektionen* and *Züge* should be filled with men who have served for a longer time.

### Shooting practice

The instructions of 3 June 1808 and 2 May 1810 emphasised the importance of shooting practice for privates and young NCOs of infantry and cavalry. New recruits would first fire a few blank rounds, to get used to the flash of the pan. Then they would fire live ammunition at 25 and 50 paces, learning the principles of aiming.

For shooting at 50 *Schritt* (37m) and 100 *Schritt* (73m), the target was to be 6 *Fuß* (188cm) high and 4 *Fuß* (125cm) wide, with a black vertical line in the middle and 12 concentric circles 10cm apart. The centre was white, the next two rings were black, and the other rings were only marked by rings. For the distances of 200 *Schritt* (146m) and 300 *Schritt* (220m), two targets were placed next to each other. An example of this target can be seen on colour plate B.

Each year, the three best marksmen of each company received awards of 1 and a half and 2 *Reichstaler* respectively. These awards were handed out in front of the company commander's quarters. On the given day, the best marksmen would march there, their shakos decorated with oak leaves, followed by the carried target, the next six best marksmen and the rest of their company, and accompanied by the regimental band.

In the *Füsilier* batallion of the *1. Schlesisches Infanterie-Regiment* the four worst marksmen of the company had to carry the target. This practice continued until 1840.

## Camps, bivouacs and billeting

On campaign, troops were generally billeted in the houses of citizens, who had to provide their food too. Alternatively, troops could set up bivouacs in the open or, if a longer stay was intended, hut camps could be built.

The size and construction of the huts was described in an instruction of 8 August 1809. The setting up of the roof of one of these huts is depicted in colour plate E.

Its base was 15 *Fuß* by 15 *Fuß* (470cm by 470cm), giving space for eight men at each side. In the middle, an empty space of 3 *Fuß* (94cm) was left, so that every man had 188cm by 59cm at his disposal for sleeping and storing his equipment, perhaps even a little more, as only 15 men should live in one hut.

On each side, four poles, each 4 *Fuß* (125cm) long and 3 *Zoll* (8cm) in diameter, were dug 2 *Fuß* (63cm) deep into the ground 150cm apart. On the top, on each side, they were connected by a row of thin beams 1.5 to 2 *Zoll* (4 to 5cm) in diameter.

The peaked roof was constructed of four thick poles on the front and back sides of the hut with eight thinner poles in between. The ends of these poles rested between the two rows of lathes on top of the side walls. Each of the poles was 10 *Fuß* (314cm) long. Each side of the roof thus had six poles with a distance of 90cm between them.

Forty-five thin beanpoles were fixed horizontally to these poles on each side. Supposing that three beanpoles were needed to cover the length of 15 Fuß (470cm), the horizontal poles would be fixed in rows about 20cm apart from each other.

Bundles of straw were bound to these poles, 'thickly enough to keep the rain off'. For one hut, 20 bundles of straw each weighing 24 *Pfund*, were provided – a total of 233kg.

The front and back walls and the small 60cm side walls were made from interwoven willow-twigs, bushes and straw. The front door was 3 *Fuß* (94cm) wide and 5 *Fuß* (157cm) high, and was made from the same materials.

With the exception of a few wooden nails, everything was bound together using only willow-twigs.

The completed hut had a height of 8 *Fuß* (251cm), and was surrounded by a small ditch. On elevated and dry ground, the side walls were only to be 1.5 *Fuß* (47cm) high and the interior dug 1 *Fuß* (31cm) deep, with the earth being used to reinforce the walls on the outside.

The huts of a battalion stood in two lines, all the doors facing the same way, to the front. The huts of the odd-numbered *Züge* were in the front row, those of the even-numbered ones in the second. The two rows were 15 *Schritt* (11m) apart, and each hut was 2 *Fuß* (63cm) apart. A distance of 9 *Fuß* (2.8m) was kept between each company. In front of the right and the left wing of each company the muskets were piled together. The battalion colours and the drums were kept in front of the middle of the battalion.

Officer of the *Garde-Regiment zu Fuß*, c. 1812. The differences between the officer's uniform and that of his men are that his coat tails are longer and he has pocket flaps with two buttons each on the back. His officer's rank is indicated by the silver tassel, the silver sash, and the officer's shoulder straps. Officers' shakos across the whole infantry bore a small eagle with a hook at each side. These eagles were silver or golden, depending on the colour of the uniform buttons, and supported a silver or golden chain. Officers' parade plumes were made from feathers. Hanging from a pocket in his trousers is a fashionable small signet attached to a pocket watch. Such items were not the preserve of the officer class alone.

Grenadier of the *Garde-Regiment zu Fuß*, c. 1812, in a contemporary engraving by Friedrich Jügel after a drawing by Ludwig Wolf. Privates of the Prussian guard infantry were named *Grenadiere*, even though they were technically *Musketiere* or *Füsiliere* and the guard regiments did not have any Grenadier companies. This regiment's dress differed from that of the line regiments in that it had white woollen lace on the collar and Swedish cuffs as well as white buttons. In addition, the *Garde-Regiment zu Fuß* had a white metal star on the shako, and on parade the men wore huge white plumes from goat hair as shown here.

15 *Schritt* (11m) behind the second line of huts were the huts of the officers, so that behind both the right and the left wing of the rank and file's huts an officer's hut could be found. The commander's hut lay directly behind the middle of the battalion.

300 *Schritt* (220m) before and 50 *Schritt* (37m) behind the middle of the battalion were the huts for the guards. The cooking fires were also located 50 *Schritt* behind the battalion. Privies were dug a decent distance in front of the battalion.

The availability of material and other conditions obviously had an impact on the construction and layout of the camp and the huts.

# EXPERIENCE OF BATTLE

### Preparing for battle

The typical proceedings and preparations prior to a battle were described by Renner in his published memoirs dated 1829: his intention was to satisfy the curiosity of young soldiers who wanted to know what war was like:

Grenadier and NCO of the *Garde-Füsilier-Bataillon*, c. 1812. Like all the Prussian *Füsiliere*, these two men are distinguished by their black belts. As an extra distinction, besides the lace on the collars and cuffs, a decree of 22 February 1810 allowed *Füsiliere* NCOs to carry a plain oval brass plate on their sabre belts. This was later suppressed by an order dated 7 May 1834.

Before the battle starts, the foremost units which have already reached the battlefield are allowed to stand at ease. The infantry piles up its arms for a short while, the cavalry dismounts. Adjutants dash along with an unusual urgency. During this period, you will move in haste from one unit to the other, looking for your good friends, talking with them not only about the pressing situation, but you will also think of your homeland, talk about dear and beloved persons there, drink their health and ask each other to convey your last farewell to them in case you should meet your death on the battlefield. On parting, friends and good comrades will clasp each others' hands more earnestly and whole-heartedly than usual. Before the beginning of the battle, some will sit or stand stoically, without fear in them. Others will be lively and will swiftly empty their bottle of spirits, and, if possible, have it filled again, before the order to commence the battle is given. Nearly everybody will try before the battle to obtain linen and bandages. Finally, the adjutants bring the orders for attack. Now you hear the vigorously and vividly called commands 'Break the piles of arms!' – 'Shoulder arms!' – 'Cavalry mount!' – 'Skirmishers advance!' Then battle will commence. The thunder of cannons resounds, the trumpets of war and the bugles join in, and with the thought of Victory or Death, every brave son of the country enters the fray.

An officer, Ludwig von Reiche, observed that sometimes soldiers who had fallen out with each other would shake hands and make peace before they went into battle. Some soldiers would pray.

The most important thing before battle was to inspect the musket and check it was working, to put a new flint in the cock and make the cartridges ready. The cartridges were transported in paper packages of 20 each (in three rows, of seven, six and seven). They were untied just before they were needed, as, due to the constant shaking caused by the soldier's movements, single cartridges in the cartridge box would lose part of their powder in the course of time.

If available, bandages and linen for first aid were distributed to the men. Some of the men would throw them away, possibly in the hope that if they did not think about being hit, they would escape.

Johann Ludwig Fischer, *Freiwilliger Jäger* in the *2. Pommersches Infanterie-Regiment*, reported that on 23 August 1813, before the Battle of Großbeeren, he 'swallowed a cartridge' (probably without the lead ball). Most of his comrades did so, too. This had been started by a few men who explained that it would prevent infection if they were wounded. It may also have stemmed from the belief that someone who already had a cartridge (or part of it) inside his body would not attract another one.

Sometimes soldiers would try to lighten the weight of their backpacks so that they could run faster in battle if need be, throwing away old shoes, books or whatever they considered unnecessary at that moment. Some who followed suit regretted it afterwards.

Some soldiers believed that playing cards would attract musket balls. Others were simpy not keen on their bodies being found with such 'sinful' (but nevertheless very common) items on them. There are many reports of the roads leading to a battlefield being strewn with playing cards, which had been thrown away by the men. Often this was done only when the first musket balls had been fired, as the men were reluctant to discard objects that would cost money to replace

Song books with far from religious content sometimes shared the same

Cartridge pouch M 1809. This item bears the oval brass plate worn on the front flap of the cartridge pouch of *Musketiere* and *Grenadiere*. Before 1807, grenadiers also had grenades in the four corners: after the reorganisaton this was meant to be discontinued. Nevertheless, there are contemporary prints of Prussian grenadiers in Paris in 1815 who display these four grenades on their cartridge pouches. Shown below is the rear view of the same item. (Blüchermuseum Kaub)

fate, as did dice. Wilhelm von Rahden, *Seconde-Lieutenant* in the *2. Schlesisches Infanterie-Regiment*, reports that the soldiers of his regiment observed a certain formality in such customs: the items had to be thrown backwards over their heads, without turning to look at them. After battle, the danger to body and soul being over, most soldiers would try to recover their playing cards and dice.

To cheer up their men and distract their minds from the imminent danger, some commanders would speak a few words before battle. To give just one example, on 16 October 1813, before attacking the village of Lindenthal near Möckern, *Major* von Krosigk galloped in front of his *Füsilier* battalion of the *2. Brandenburgisches Infanterie-Regiment* and shouted:

'Brave men of war! The hour has come, prepare for battle. All of you are fighting for one aim alone: the freedom of Europe. All for one, one for all. With this war-cry let righteous battle commence. We shall take the village here in front of us by storm.'

### The first battle

On 27 September 1812 Karl Renner, *Musketier* in the 1st Battalion of the *2. Westpreußisches Infanterie-Regiment*, saw combat for the first time:

About a quarter of a mile south of Eckau our infantry formed up behind a small piece of rising ground. When this had been done, we put the muskets together and we were allowed to rest a while, as we had been marching all the night until then, shortly before noon. In front of our battalion, on the rising ground a battery had unlimbered. In order to watch the deployment of the enemy, many curious soldiers ran to the top of this rising ground, I among them. We had been looking for only a few minutes, when we saw in the distance some smoke rise up, and almost at the same moment a cannon ball passed above us with a loud buzzing. Our artillery, which had been waiting ready for action on this rising ground (which we immediately vacated), replied to the kind invitation of the enemy. The command 'Gewehr in die Hand!' [Take up arms!] was given. … But the enemy cannon continued as before, starting to bring death and destruction among us, which caused fear and terror among the young soldiers, who tried to escape the imminent danger by ducking down. A soon as our brave battalion commander, *Major* von Löbell (now [in 1829] General-Major), saw this, he coolly rode up and down our front, as if on the parade ground. Several other officers showed the same calmness and fearlessness, especially our brave company commander, *Kapitain* von Rohr (now *Oberst* and commander of the 26. *Infanterie-Regiment*), and the adjutant of our battalion, *Lieutenant* von Legat (now *Oberst* in the Ministry of War). This display made us so proud that nobody thought any more of ducking, even though the buzzing of the balls became more and more intense.

We had stood there a few minutes, and the command was shouted '*Tirailleure vor!*' [Skirmishers advance!] The bugler blew for the first section to deploy as skirmishers. In front of us there was a thicket of birch and alder trees, encircled by a shallow and dry ditch with a thin fence, which we used for cover. We had just arrived at this place, when the enemy bullets began whizzing above us in massed volleys, and here and there one of them punched through the tiny fence, oblivious to the fact that it was our sole protection. We couldn't not respond to the enemy, so we sent bullets back to them, but were not able to make out if a few of them achieved their aim. The enemy skirmishers who were hidden in the undergrowth were most discontent with our counter-greeting, they came out of the forest, shouting 'Hurrah!', and in a number so superior to ours that they forced us to leave our position. The retreat was performed with the greatest precision, and as only a few were wounded, the whole affair seemed to have been but an exercise on the parade ground. Now, in our first engagement, we had convinced ourselves that the banging and whizzing of bullets would not bear inevitable death, but that above us, in front of us, at our sides and behind us there was plenty of space to cause them to miss us.

Not everybody described their first action as cheerfully as Renner. *Füsilier* Hechel of the *2. Brandenburgisches Infanterie-Regiment* was much less reluctant to reveal his inner feelings. His memoirs were not written down in order to be read by a wider public, but intended for himself and his family, and published more than 10 years after his death. Hechel's first battle was the crossing of the River Elbe at Wartenburg on 3 October 1813:

It was the first time in my life and my heart was beating against my ribs, so that I believed the man at my side must hear it. But he didn't feel any better. There we had Wartenburg in front of us, and a single small dam of the River Elbe led towards it, raked by the enemy batteries. The cannon balls were buzzing above us. Now the order was given: '*Patronen los!*' ['Ready cartridges!'] The packages were untied and 60 cartridges poured in the cartridge box. The command '*Geladen!*' ['Load!'] was shouted, and at our sides, before and behind us shells fell down. One crushed the attendant of our *Kapitain,* others tore big branches from the trees and passed through the undergrowth. Now all my limbs were trembling, the hair on my head bristled and I believed it would lift my shako high into the air. I looked around, but whoever I looked at, he was trembling too. I have little to tell about my first battle. My confusion was still too strong. Also, the *Leib-Regiment* stood in front of us in the line of fire and had to bear the strongest thrust. To reach the dam of the River Elbe, we had to cross a swamp in a shower of bullets. Many of those before us fell, but we bravely shot back. Behind the dam, we found French soldiers. Beside them, they had heaps of already bitten off cartridges, for reloading faster. Those of them who could run, ran. But many stayed, all of them had been wounded in the head, as the rest of their bodies had been protected by the dam. Besides the cartridges, the enemy had also left pots and cauldrons full of plum soup. We took hold of it and ate in the midst of the heaviest musketry fire. So much had our fear left us, none of us surely would have touched a mouthful when first under fire. Now the famous lighting attack by *General* Horn followed, all along the narrow dam of the River Elbe, onto the enemy cannons and in the middle of the village Wartenburg. The *Leib-Regiment* was attacking in front of us – I was, as told, still too confused and don't know myself how I reached the end of the dam. We moved along over the littered corpses of our comrades. When I recovered my senses, the enemy had already been put to flight and the glorious day, which was the cause for *General* von Yorck's honorary surname 'von Wartenburg', came to an end.

Most soldiers agreed that the more battles they took part in, the more they lost their fear. But there are others whose feelings were different. *Lieutenant* Kretzschmer of the 1st battalion (raised in the Pomeranian town Anklam) of the *2. Kurmärkisches Landwehr-Infanterie-Regiment* narrates his experience:

Many describe their feelings during their first action as anxious, and are convinced that the more often men are fired upon, the better

Drawing of the cartridge pouch's brass plate with a trophy decoration. The dimensions of surviving originals vary from 12.4cm by 10.6cm over 12.1cm by 10.5cm to 12cm by 11cm. (Jakob Ziegert)

they get used to the conditions and become familiar with the danger. But for me, it was the opposite. With good cheer, and with high enthusiasm, full of eagerness to give battle with the French [he led his men into his first action]. Finally, the long awaited moment had come to look the hated enemy in the eye … But this cheerfulness diminished with time, the more often I entered combat, the more I became aware of the dangers awaiting the soldier. After a few times, as we marched out I would think: 'if only today the bitter cup would pass and we do not give battle' or, if we were already in combat: 'if only today the sun would set a little faster, so that the thing would come to an end' … Those who say they would go into battle as readily as a dance are but bragging! At least for me, it was so only during my first battle, later my reflections before battle became more and more serious. … Let this confession of what went on inside me and which God alone can know for sure, be received not as one of a coward, because I have never been one, but as one of a lover of the truth. And I do believe that the bravery of a man who does his part out of a sense of duty is worth much more than the foolhardiness of a braggard who doesn't know himself.

**Rules of war**

Renner in his memoirs, which were also meant to serve for the instruction of young soldiers, refers to the following rules of war:

> The expression 'war' denotes in international law the status between independent nations, in which these pursue their rights with force. The rules of war of civilised nations do not allow at all that prisoners of war are killed or hurt. Their captor is only allowed to take possession of their property. Often the prisoners, especially the officers, are released on parole, not to serve again before they have been formally exchanged, and to present themselves whenever it is demanded. Anybody breaking his parole, when caught, will be treated as a deserter without honour. Spies and marauders (those soldiers who singly or in groups, without orders of their officers, dare to commit violent or hostile acts against the inhabitants) cannot claim to be treated as prisoners of war, usually they will be sentenced to death without a long trial. During negotiations in times of war, bearers of a flag of truce as well as guards left behind to protect individuals or their property are to be treated as inviolable.

These may have been (or should have been) the accepted rules during the Napoleonic Wars, but they applied only to those who were already recognised as prisoners. There was no right of the defeated to be taken prisoner. The unspoken and unwritten rule was that an enemy soldier who entered the battlefield had forfeited his life. Whether he kept his life or not depended on the mercy of the victorious troops. This was fair and in that it applied equally to both sides. We find many references to battles in which quarter was 'neither given nor sought' by Prussian soldiers (and their adversaries). Much, of course, depended on the individual soldier's character and psychological state.

Preparing the greatcoat for carrying it rolled over the shoulder was best done with the help of comrades, in this case those of the re-enacted *Leib-Infanterie-Regiment*. The greatcoat was spread out (note the linen lining) and then the outer parts were folded inwards.

The greatcoat was then rolled up, starting from the top. Finally, the two ends were bound together and the roll was ready to be slung over the left shoulder. British and French army greatcoats of the period were cut differently from the Prussian ones, their circumference at the bottom being much smaller. Men who were equipped with them could not carry them rolled over the shoulder, as the roll was not long enough.

One of the days where quarter was not given was 16 October 1813. In the afternoon the *Füsilier* battalion of the *2. Brandenburgisches Infanterie-Regiment*, which formed part of the 8th brigade commanded by *General-Lieutenant* von Hünerbein, joined the general attack of this brigade on a French battery, which was supported by three battalions in column. (Although all the reports use the word '*Quarrée*' (then the German word for square), this probably just refers to the shape of the formation.)

The battery was taken, but with heavy losses. *Major* von Krosigk, the battalion's beloved and lion-hearted commander, was killed when he attacked one of the supporting French battalions on his own, without waiting for his men. Hechel reports:

We saw this and rushed after him. When we reached the column, it had closed its ranks again, but the enemy troops were trembling all over. I had pressed forward and stood just in front of their bayonets, but had to rest for a moment first. Then *Unteroffizier* Böttcher and I turned our muskets, first to beat aside their levelled bayonets with our butts and then to swipe at their faces. Our comrades followed our example, and even today I cannot understand why the enemy stood so densely packed and did not defend themselves. They let themselves be slain without resistance, or crawled away. But then we would beat them more, and even though they begged '*Pardon, Kamerad!*' ['Quarter, comrade!'] our cruel answer was '*Nixs Pardon!*' [literally 'Nothing quarter!' – imitating the rudimentary German of the French], until the whole column had been wiped out.

Even non-combatants were not spared. Hechel continues:

Now we went on to the second column. When we were in the thick of it, a French doctor jumped up to run away, but my comrade Busch, son of a school teacher, who stood at my side, chased after him and stabbed his bayonet into his side so that he fell. When Busch drew back his musket, the bayonet was stuck. He shouted "Alas, now I don't have a musket!" because the doctor, who died immediately, was lying on the side where the bayonet was embedded." I said: "There are enough muskets lying around here, just take another one!" He did, and we bravely continued to fight.

Hechel shows no sign of reproach or remorse (except for having made the musket unusable). It was considered 'normal' under the circumstances of this battle. The fighting continued:

'Still there was one French column in the distance. A French officer came towards us from it, waving a white handkerchief. It was an angry day. We did not give and did not seek quarter. So we took no notice of this sign of peace and answered with bullets. The officer fell, his column fled. Many found refuge in the nearby forest, but we did not spare anyone that came within our reach. Finally, night fell.'

Fortunately these 'angry days' were not common, and were probably only caused by heavy losses. Hechel, who incidentally was quite a religious person, usually treated the prisoners he took relatively kindly.

However, in his memoirs he never expressed any remorse for what happened near Möckern on that day. In addition there do not appear to be any references to a Prussian soldier of that period being reprimanded for having killed a would-be prisoner. Such rules of conduct seem deeply at odds with our modern standards of humanity.

### Communication in battle

The most important means of transferring orders on the battlefield was the voice of the commanding officer. It was important that he could speak loudly and clearly enough to be understood with ease, and that he was calm, to breed confidence in his men.

Usually the men could recognise and distinguish the voice of their commanding officer. If they did not, the results could be fatal, as demonstrated by the following incident during the Battle of Dennewitz on 6 September 1813.

*Major* von Wittich had taken over command of the 2nd battalion of the *3. Reserve-Infanterie-Regiment* on 29 August. He had 'an excellent voice for command', but had not yet had the chance to exercise the whole battalion together before this battle, so that not all the men knew his voice. His battalion was advancing towards the enemy in attack column, muskets already in their right hands and in good spirits, when *Major* von Wittich gave the command '*Halb links!*' (move towards the left front). Part of the men performed '*Links um*' (left about), a part continued to move on correctly towards the left front and others stopped, having heard '*Halt*' (stop). The ranks collided and several men began shouting at each other and asking 'what was the command?' Others responded, repeating the different commands they believed they had heard. The

A group of officers from different units in 1812 or 1813, in a contemporary print by Ludwig Wolf. Note the height of the officer of the regiment Garde du Corps compared to that of his fellow officers. The identity of the fourth man from the left is unknown, his headgear does not match any Prussian regulation uniform of the period. (Kupferstichkabinett Berlin)

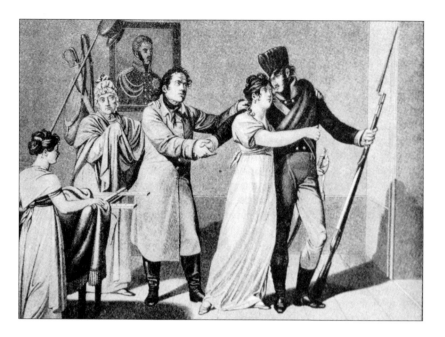

Departure of the soldier for war, in a popular print of the period. It seems common that a print of the Prussian king adorned the walls of patriotic households.

following *Züge* collided with the two front *Züge*, the ranks intermingled, and at the same time the battalion received blasts of cannister from the front and cannon shot from the flank. This increased the confusion and a few men turned about, expecting the order to retreat. So the battalion 'had to be led back', together with the other two battalions of the regiment who had joined the attack, and re-formed while screened by some of the skirmishers from the 2nd battalion.

The regimental history's conclusion from this incident was as follows: 'The best advice seems to be not to test the tactical abilities of the men with unfamiliar movements when they are close to the enemy.'

During skirmishing, when the men were too widely spread out to be commanded by voice, the bugle was used for giving commands. The 1812 regulation prescribed short signals for each different part of the battalion (deployed skirmishers, supporting troops, each of the four companies and the whole battalion) which were to be combined with signals for all the basic movements, e.g 'skirmishers – cease fire' or '3rd Company – deploy as skirmishers'.

Wilhelm Häring, a *Freiwilliger Jäger* in the *Colbergsches Infanterie-Regiment*, provides details of his skirmisher training in May and June 1815:

'I realised that for me, being unmusical, the signals of the bugles were difficult to remember. But I was not the only one, and I was consoled by the assurance veterans gave to me, that in combat this would not matter much, that in the thundering of the cannons and the heat of skirmishing, the call of the bugle would not be listened to. Everybody would jump, shoot, run and turn as he would think best for him and where he would expect to hit the enemy.'

One should add that most soldiers would follow what the majority of their comrades did, if they realised that they had not heard the command.

It would be interesting to know what Häring's commanding officer would have thought of this veteran's advice. But even though Häring has a tendency to ridicule military matters in this way, the above would certainly have applied for many of the Prussian skirmishers who were still green. Naturally, the more experienced or better trained skirmishers would have been much better at responding to the commands of their officer. After all, this was the purpose of training.

### Standing in reserve

In action, whether the men had to stand to attention all the time when they were in reserve, or whether they were allowed to rest and sit down, seems to have depended on the will of the battalion or regimental commander. On 16 October 1813, the *11. Reserve-Infanterie-Regiment* was formed up under arms for two hours, awaiting an order to attack the village of Markkleeberg, and the men became very tired. *Kapitain* von Busse of this regiment, which was renamed *23. Infanterie-Regiment* in spring 1815, comments:

> The careful treatment of ones troops, provided that it is not to the disadvantage of military service, is one of the most important duties of the commander. Therefore it is unjust and vindictive to have infantry stand under arms for hours, when it is formed up in attack column and gathered for battle, in reserve or as protection for a battery. In such cases the infantry may be allowed, provided there are no objections nor danger of the enemy surprising them, to open the *Züge* and ranks of the columns and let the officers and men sit down. The latter should keep their muskets upright in their hands, with the butts of the muskets on the ground. In a sitting position, the infantry is also much less exposed to losses from enemy cannon fire. This was experienced by the two *Musketier* battalions of the 23. *Infanterie-Regiment* (who had been allowed to sit down, in the Battle of Ligny [16 June 1815], on the heights of Bussy).

The regimental commander of the *11. Reserve-Infanterie-Regiment* in 1813 was *Oberst* von Schwichow. When he became commander of the fortress of Minden in April 1815, his successor was *Oberst* von Wienskowski. Both had started their careers in the 'old Prussian' army prior to 1806.

### Cowardice and taking cover

*Major* Count Reichenbach of the *2. Schlesisches Infanterie-Regiment* called out to his men in the Battle of Großgörschen on 2 May 1813: 'Men! The bullets you hear whistling will not hit you. Therefore, it is useless to fear them. Let nobody dare to duck!'

Most soldiers held ducking and similar acts of seeking cover in disdain. In the 1st Company of the *1. Pommersches Infanterie-Regiment* the tallest man, who stood on the right of the first rank, was *Musketier* Ott. His younger brother had joined his company as a recruit shortly before and stood in the second rank behind him. In the action at Hoyerswerda on 28 May 1813, the company had to hold out under enemy fire for some time, and several of the soldiers, including the younger brother, tried to duck down when the musket balls passed close by. His brother ordered him not to, explaining

Kapitain Leopold August Eduard von Reckow, between 1809 and 1811. Born on 7 February 1769, he became a cadet on 26 May 1776. In 1787 he entered military service in the infantry and was promoted to *Kapitain* in the *Colbergsches Infanterie-Regiment* on 20 August 1808. On 1 January 1812, he rose to the rank of Major, commanding the *Füsilier-Bataillon*, until he was transfered to be commander of the 9. *Reserve-Infanterie-Regiment* on 11 August 1813. His favourite words to encourage his men were: 'Trust in God and do not despair, children.' After some time, the officers of the 9. *Reserve-Infanterie-Regiment* started to call him 'Zage nicht' ('do not despair'): the men picked this up and in the end the whole regiment was known by other units as 'die Zage nichts' ('the never-despairing ones'). He died in 1835.

**Füsilier of the *Leichtes Bataillon* of the *Colbergsches Infanterie-Regiment*, December 1808**

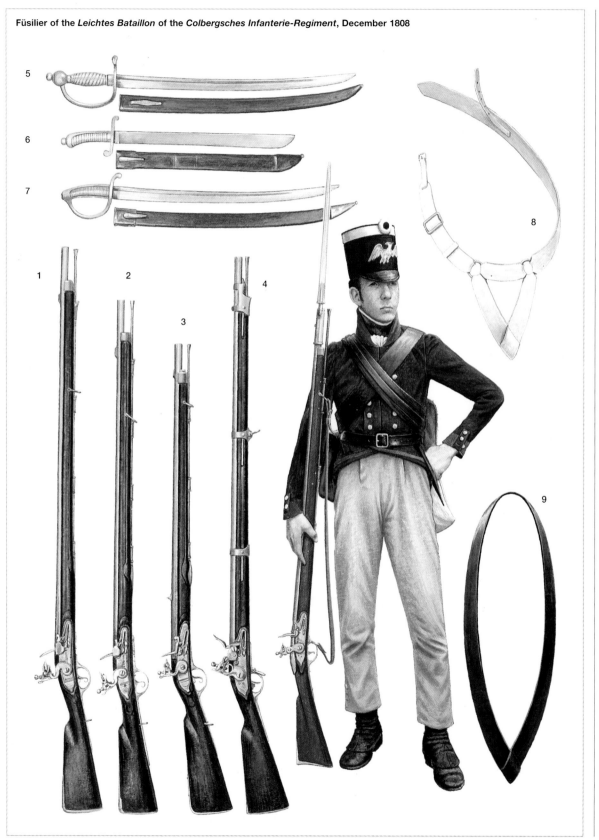

**A**

**B**

A group of soldiers of the *Füsilier-Bataillon* of the *Colbergsches Infanterie-Regiment* on shooting exercise, summer 1811

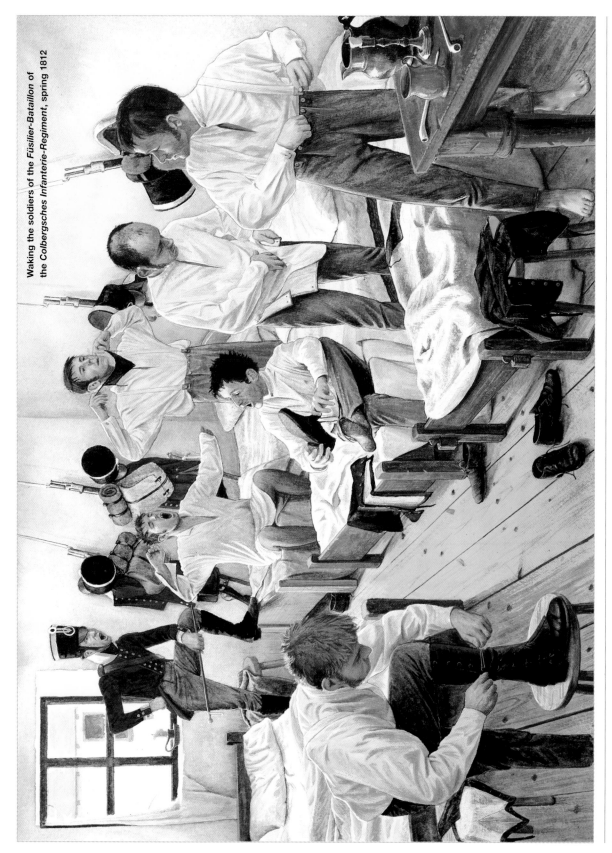

Waking the soldiers of the *Füsilier-Bataillon* of the *Colbergsches Infanterie-Regiment*, spring 1812

C

The 2. *Pommersches Reserve-Bataillon* forms an attack column from the line near the village of Grabow, 12 May 1813

**D**

The *Füsilier-Bataillon* of the *9. Reserve-Infanterie-Regiment* sets up camp close to Schadewalde near the fortress of Wittenberg, 13 September 1813

E

The *Füsilier-Bataillon* of the *9. Reserve-Infanterie-Regiment* skirmishing on the morning of the Battle of Laon, on the slope above the village Ardon, 9 March 1814

F

Men of the *Füsilier-Bataillon* of the *21. Infanterie-Regiment* during the storming of Medy-bas, 15 September 1815

G

***Feldwebel* of the *Füsilier-Bataillon* of the *21. Infanterie-Regiment*, October 1815**

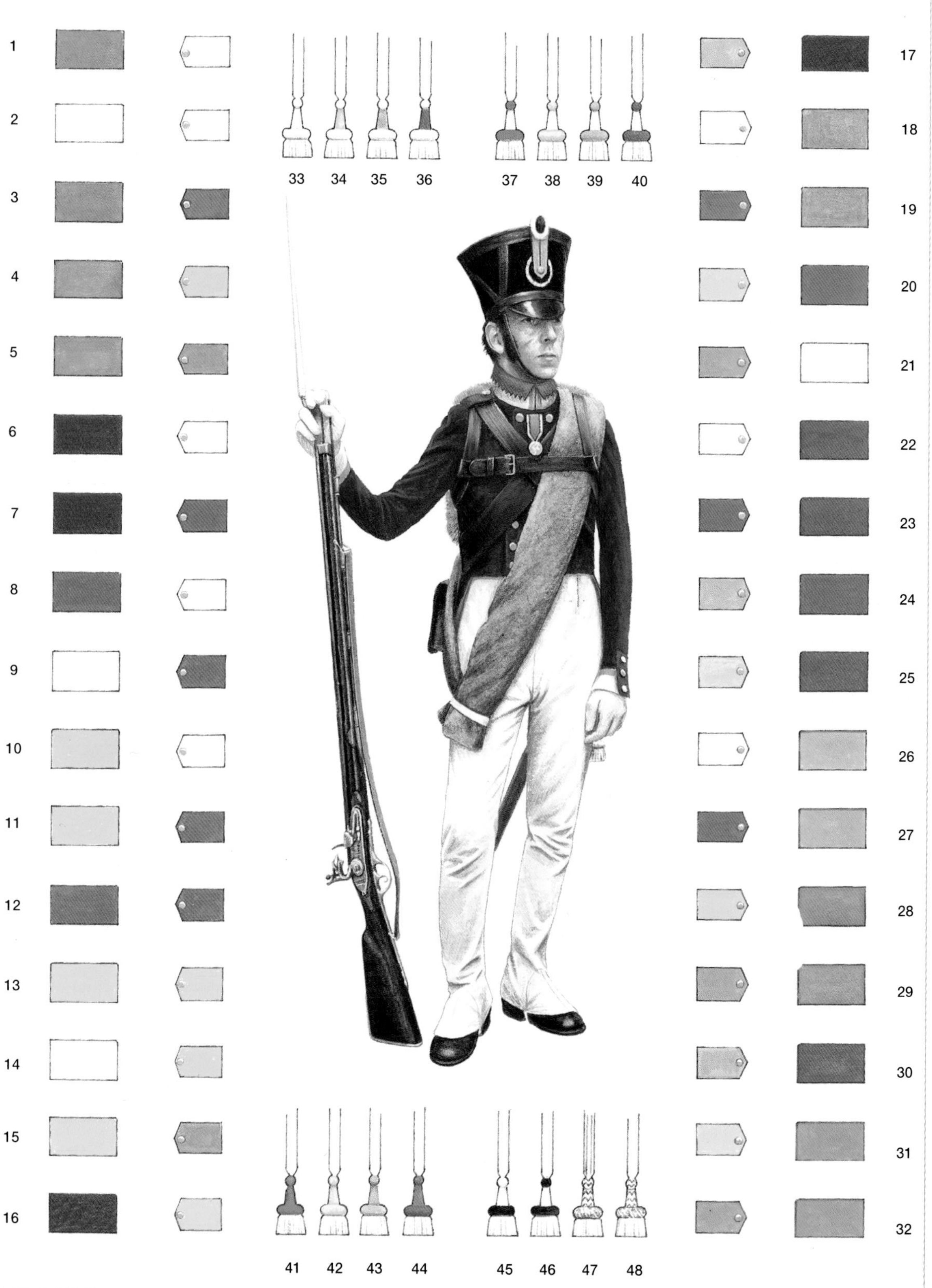
1
2
3
4
5
6
7
8
9
10
11
12
13
14
15
16
17
18
19
20
21
22
23
24
25
26
27
28
29
30
31
32
33
34
35
36
37
38
39
40
41
42
43
44
45
46
47
48

**H**

that it would be improper, unsoldierly and pointless. For some time the younger Ott obeyed, but when the enemy fire became more intense, he forgot his brothers admonition. Seeing this, the man behind him in the third rank called out to the older brother: 'Ott! Your brother keeps on ducking!' Ott turned, took his brother by the collar and gave him a harsh clip around the ear, with the words: 'Look! The balls won't do half this damage!' Apparently this had an effect, and the younger Ott never ducked again in enemy fire.

For skirmishers, the rules were not as strict. Füsiliere Hechel of the *2. Brandenburgisches Infanterie-Regiment* reports of the action at Möckern on 16 October 1813:

'At our side, our *Major* [von Krosigk] stopped and studied the enemy. Suddenly, he ordered "Füsiliere, throw yourself down, these dogs will fire at any moment." But they didn't fire.'

### Preventing a rout

In the action at Zahna on 5 September 1813, the 1st battalion of the *3. Reserve-Infanterie-Regiment* had to retreat in line for a short distance, being pressed from behind by enemy skirmishers. Several soldiers broke rank and started running. The battalion's commander, Major von Welling, realised such an example could spell danger for the inexperienced men of his battalion. He ordered the battalion to make front towards the enemy again (an orderly retreat was usually done by ordering a 'turn about') and had a battalion volley fired. The enemy stopped their pursuit, and Major von Welling explained to his men that they were retreating and not fleeing, and that he would shoot the next man to leave his rank through the head. He pulled out his pistol and ordered 'turn about' and 'march'. The enemy pressed on, one *Musketier* broke ranks and was shot by von Welling. This had the desired effect, and the battalion slowly continued on its retreat without any more disorder arising.

Major von Welling was entitled to do so by paragraph 16 of the Articles of War: 'The soldier who first takes to flight in the face of the enemy, under any circumstances whatsoever, may be shot directly. The same punishment will befall him later, if it cannot be done at once.'

Usually, officers who wanted to prevent or stop a rout tried to prevent individuals from running away by beating them with their sabres, using the flat side and not the sharp edge.

# LEAVING MILITARY SERVICE

There were several ways of leaving the field army; desertion, invalidity and other ways of governmental maintenance, and dismissal. The last method became the most common after the period of military service had been reduced to three years in 1814.

Prussian infantrymen resting on the march, between 1810 and 1813, in a contemporary print by Ludwig Wolf. They have found some straw to lie on: in the background one man seems to have made a fire. Note the stuffed backpack of the man sitting in the front. (Kupferstichkabinett Berlin)

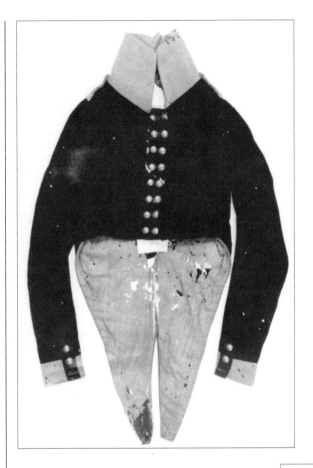

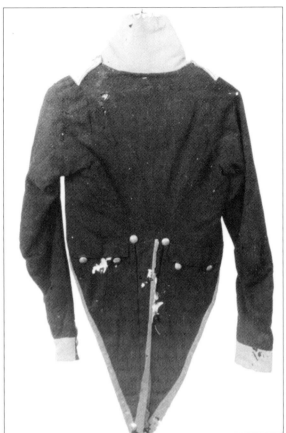

ABOVE **Uniform coat of Albrecht von Gültlingen in 1809. He lived from 1774 to 1828 and was *Premier-Lieutenant* in the *1. Ostpreußisches Infanterie-Regiment* from 24 March 1809 to 20 February 1810. Typical of Prussian uniforms in this period are the high waistline, the very narrow shoulders (the shoulder joints were covered by the cloth of the sleeves), the very small distance between the two rows of buttons and the narrow cuffs (here 2 *Zoll*, 5.2cm). The cuff flaps are 8cm long. (Wehrgeschichtliches Museum Rastatt)**

ABOVE RIGHT **Rear view. The white spots are lining showing through the cloth of the uniform which has been eaten by moths. The pockets in the coat tails are accessible through openings in the two back folds below the waist buttons. The pocket flaps have no function. The buttons at the fold of the turnbacks are non-regulation.**

RIGHT **Inside view. There is a pocket in the left breast of the coat, 12cm wide and 17cm deep. The breast lining is of dark blue cloth, the lining in the back as well as in the sleeves is linen. The coat tails are lined with cheap red cloth, the red turnbacks on the outside are of better quality. Both sides of the breast are filled with padding, which is up to 4cm thick.**

## Desertion

Due to the better treatment of soldiers and the end of recruiting *Ausländer*, desertion was no longer a serious problem in the Prussian army after 1807. Most desertions were committed by soldiers who came from the Polish-speaking parts of Silesia and West Prussia. In 1815, when many conscripts from newly acquired provinces were taken into the army, the desertion rate rose. Most of these conscripts had formerly been soldiers in the French and Confederation of the Rhine armies.

To give an example, on 11 May 1815 the *24. Infanterie-Regiment* received reinforcements of 523 men from the Lower Rhine, who were distributed to the companies. Several men were invalids and had to be sent back, about 30 or 40 were transferred to the artillery or as cadre to the Rhine *Landwehr*, but of the rest 93 deserted in May and June. After the battles of Ligny and Belle-Alliance (Waterloo), another 101 of them were missing, most of them were believed by the regiment to have deserted. The regimental commander, Major von Laurens, was so upset by this fact that from that point on he sometimes added the following words to official requests for decoration for those reinforcements who had stayed with the regiment: 'Though he is a Rhinelander, he is worth the bravest of the regiment.'

## Invalidity

An *AKO* of 18 November 1808 ordered that soldiers who had served without blemish and who now lacked the strength necessary for field service but wanted to stay in the military at the end of their term, could enter the regimental garrison company until they qualified as invalids.

Certain preconditions regarding the privileges of invalids were laid down by the *AKO* of 14 March 1811. Invalids were grouped into two categories: semi-invalids who were unfit for field service, but could still perform garrison duty, and full invalids who were neither fit for field service nor for garrison service. Unless they could claim to have served with a clean record or to have distinguished themselves, soldiers did not hold the right to be acknowledged as invalids.

The advantage of joining a garrison or invalids' company was that the soldiers continued to be provided with the basics of life: food, accommodation and clothing.

Men belonging to any of the following categories were acknowleged as semi- invalids and could be transfered to a garrison company:

1 those who had been wounded in combat and were thus unfit for field service
2 those who had been disabled whilst on duty
3 those awarded the *Militair-Ehrenzeichen* decoration
4 NCOs who had become unfit for field service during their military service after six years, privates after eight years of service;
5 NCOs who had become unfit for field service due to reasons beyond their military service after 12 years, privates after 26 years of service.

Full invalids, who had the right to enter a company of invalids, were:

1 those who had become unfit for military service due to wounds or disabilities suffered on duty
2 NCOs after 21 years, and privates after 28 years, of active military service.

Those who did not qualify to be cared for by the government were dismissed and joined the other destitute poor of their native towns or districts. For the *Ausländer* among them who had served without blemish, arrangements would be made 'to somehow provide them with the most necessary means of living'.

Semi or full invalidity did not mean necessarily that the men were unable to earn their living. Hechel, who had been severely wounded in the battle at Belle-Alliance on 18 June 1815 and had been in hospital for nearly a year, was declared a full invalid in 1816, and was allowed to join the *1. Provinzial-Invaliden-Kompanie* in the town of Brandenburg:

'Besides my invalid's salary, which did not go very far, I earned what I needed through the work of my hands and made a good living. My additional income was so good, that sometimes I made one *Reichstaler* per day. I carted bricks from the kiln day and night, or carried grass from the islands in the River Havel, often having to wade up to my trunk in the water. I avoided no work, mainly because I wanted to test my body to see whether it was capable of hard work. Thanks to God, it stood every test.'

Some men were granted allowances, which were not sufficient to pay a man's living, but at least served as a contribution to the costs. Monthly allowances were 3 *Reichstaler* for a *Feldwebel*, 2 for an *Unteroffizier* and 1 for a private. If a soldier preferred to receive the allowance instead of holding a position in a company of invalids, his allowance could be a bit higher. Those eligible for allowances were:

1 soldiers who had been wounded in the field or disabled on duty, but had not become fully unable to work

2 those fully unable to work and who had served for at least 8 years (if they were NCOs) or 12 years (privates)

3 those who had served without blemish for 18 years (NCOs) or 24 years (privates).

Members of the two last categories could claim no right to receive allowances, unless they had been awarded the *Militair-Ehrenzeichen* (the military badge of honour, given to privates and NCOs for bravery before 1808 and replaced by the Iron Cross in 1813). *Militair-Ehrenzeichen* awardees enjoyed other advantages too.

Invalids who had 'served well' could receive a *Versorgungsschein* (guarantee of civil employment), which entitled them to be employed by the government – if they met the qualifications necessary for the position. Full invalids who renounced their position in a company of invalids, or those who renounced their allowances, could receive such a guarantee as well. Hechel commented:

Detail of the officer's shoulder strap, which has also been eaten by moths. It is made from red cloth, covered with white cloth (to identify the 1st regiment of the province), to which the officer's lace (of silver, black and white thread) is sewn. The button is sewn to the shoulder strap and shoulder and cannot be unbuttoned. Another typical feature of Prussian uniforms of this period is that the shoulder strap overlaps the collar slightly. The shoulder straps of the rank and file could be unbuttoned.

'Such a guarantee of civil employment is like the key which opens the gate to future happiness. You hold it in your hand, but you don't yet know where to put it.'

He received such a guarantee, obtained leave to study at a teachers' seminary for one year, and used his guarantee to become a school teacher in the town of Brandenburg in 1819.

### Discharge

Soldiers or *Kantonisten* who wished to be discharged before completing their time of service, had to get the consent of the brigade commander. Their request would be considered and decided on once a year, at the time when the new recruits were selected. In special circumstances, men were allowed to request their discharge during other times of the year too, for example, when getting married or after receiving an inheritance which increased the wealth of the applicant to an amount which made him a member of the class of men exempted from military duty. In times of war, discharge was not granted.

Usually discharge was granted following the completion of the set period of service. Wilhelm von Rahden, Lieutenant in the *2. Schlesisches Infanterie-Regiment*, gives us a touching description of the discharge of veterans from his regiment in 1816, who after three years in the military now returned to civilian life:

> I still remember – even though nearly a lifetime has gone by since then – the formation of the company. After the official part our *Kapitain* von Korth had us wheel in to form a circle and with a few rousing words he thanked and bade farewell to the brave ones who left us forever. Yes, some of them he even approached and shook their offered hands. We younger officers, on the other hand, let our feelings show. As soon as the *Kapitain* had departed, we hugged our sincere, brave and loyal comrades in battle, and accompanied them for half an hour, until far beyond the glacis of the fortress. Thierig played a last time on his violin, and the men sang along with his melancholy tune. Probst spoke the valediction. And now the last farewell. Then we gazed after our old comrades for a long time, with deep sadness.

# GLOSSARY

**AKO** *Allerhöchste Kabinetts-Order* – Order by the 'Highest [Royal] Cabinet', a law issued by the King.

**Ausländer** A foreigner who was not a subject of the Prussian state. This included people from other German states, e.g. Saxons, Bavarians, etc.

**Feldwebel** Sergeant major.

**Freiwilliger Jäger** Volunteer rifleman, equipping himself at his own cost and serving in a special company of *Freiwillige Jäger* attached to a battalion.

**Füsilier** In the Prussian army, a soldier of the regimental light battalion.

**Fuß** also: *Rheinländischer Fuß* 31.374cm. Basic unit of length measurement in the main Prussian provinces from 28 October 1773. 1 *Fuß* consisted of 12 *Zoll*, each *Zoll* consisted of 12 *Linien*, making 144 *Linien* per *Fuß*.

**Groschen** See *Reichstaler*.**Hauptmann** See *Kapitain*.

**Hautboist** Musician of the regimental band.

**Hornist** Bugler.

**Kanton** Recruiting canton.

**Kantonist** A man in the *Kanton* not selected for military service, but still liable for it in principle.

**Kapitain** Captain. This rank was often also called *Hauptmann*.

**Krümper** A man belonging to the regimental reserve in the *Kanton*, who could be called up by his regiment at any time.

**Kapitain d' armes** The Unteroffizier within the company who is in charge of equipment and distributions

**Landrat** District magistrate.

**Landwehr** (literally country defence) Units created from men aged 25 to 40, too old to be recruits for the field army. The responsibility for the formation and equipment of the *Landwehr* was given to the provincial authorities instead of the ministry of war.

**Leichtes Bataillon** Light Batallion. Denomination of *Füsilier* battalions before 1 December 1809.

**Linie** 2.179mm. See *Fuß*.

**Musketier** In the Prussian army, a soldier of the regimental line battalions.

**Oberst** Colonel.

**Pfennig** See *Reichstaler*.

**Pfund** Pound: 485.36g.

**Portion** Daily food ration for one man.

**Quart** Equivalent to 1.1449 litres.

**Ration** Daily food ration for a horse.

**Regiments-Chef** Regimental commander. In the period dealt with in this book, an honorary position only.

**Reichstaler** [also: Taler] Official currency in Prussia. 1 *Reichstaler* consisted of 24 *Groschen*, each *Groschen* consisted of 12 *Pfennig*, making 288 *Pfennig* per *Reichstaler*.

**Schritt** According to regulations 1 *Schritt* measured 2 *Fuß* 4 *Zoll*, the equivalent of 73.22cm.

**Sektion** Section of a *Zug* consisting of 5 or 6 rows.

**Spielmann** [pl. *Spielleute*] Literally, 'a man who plays [an instrument]', i.e. a drummer or bugler.

**Taler** See *Reichstaler*.

**Tambour** Drummer.

**Unteroffizier** Sergeant. In a broader sense, it also means NCO, i.e. sergeant or sergeant major.

**Zoll** 2.615cm. See *Fuß*.

**Zug** Platoon, half a company.

# COLLECTIONS, MUSEUMS AND RE-ENACTMENT

The images in this book credited *Kupferstichkabinett Berlin* are from the Kupferstichkabinett, Staatliche Museen zu Berlin – Preußischer Kulturbesitz. Copyright: Bildarchiv Preußischer Kulturbesitz, Berlin, 2001. Photographer: Jörg P. Anders, Berlin, 2001.

Many of the photographs of surviving original items are from the collections of the following two museums:

**Blücher Museum in Kaub**

*www.rhein-lahn-info.de/kaub/museum/bluechermuseum.htm*

and:

*www.befreiungskriege.de/bluecher_museum.htm*

Franz Xavier von Korff, *Seconde-Lieutenant* of *Füsiliere* in the 12th company of the *1. Pommersches Infanterie-Regiment*, killed in the storming of Leipzig on 19 October 1813. He was born in April 1784 and became an officer in the *Infanterie-Regiment von Ruits* (No. 8) in 1805. The shoulder straps are those for *Lieutenants* between 23 October 1808 and 18 June 1812. The high collar indicates an early date for this portrait. (Collection Vetterling)

**Wehrgeschichtliches Museum in Rastatt**
*www.wgm-rastatt.de*
The remnants of the former collection of the Zeughaus in Berlin are now part of:
**Deutsches Historisches Museum, Berlin**
*www.dhm.de*

Other museums which exhibit Prussian items of the Napoleonic period are:
**Militärhistorisches Museum, Dresden**
*www.milhistmuseum.de*
**Bayrisches Armeemuseum, Ingolstadt**
*www.bayerisches-armeemuseum.de*

If you are interested in re-enacting the Prussian line infantry, the following organisations are recommended:
**1. Pommersches Infanterie-Regiment**
*www.befreiungskriege.de/preussen1815.htm*
**Leib-Infanterie-Regiment**
*www.mitglied.tripod.de/ThiloS/Brandenburg/Leibinfanterie.htm*

# BIBLIOGRAPHY AND FURTHER READING

Additional notes and corrections regarding the subject matter of this book can be found at the author's personal website:
*www.the-prussian-eagle.de*

The following English books on the organisation of the Prusian armies of the Napoleonic Wars are recommended:
Shanahan, W., *Prussian Military Reforms 1786–1813*, New York, 1945
Paret, P., *Yorck and the Era of Prussian Reform*, Princeton, NJ, 1966
Nafziger, George F., *The Prussian Army during the Napoleonic Wars (1792–1815)*, 3 vols, West Chester, Ohio, 1996

The most important works, quoting original sources, on the Prussian army from 1808 to 1815 are:
Vaupel, Rudolf, *Das Preussische Heer vom Tilsiter Frieden bis zur Befreiung 1807–1814*, Leipzig, 1938. (Unfortunately, only vol. 1, covering 1807 and 1808, has been published.)
Scherbening und von Willisen, *Die Reorganisation der Preußischen Armee nach dem Tilsiter Frieden*, 2 vols, Berlin, 1862–1866
German General Staff, *Das Preussische Heer der Befreiungskriege*, 3 vols, Berlin, 1912, 1914, 1920
Jany, Curt, *Geschichte der Königlich Preußischen Armee, – Vol. 4: Die Königlich Preußische Armee und das Deutsche Reichsheer 1807 bis 1914*, Berlin, 1933
Beeger, Friedrich Wilhelm, *Seltsame Schicksale, eines allen Soldaten*, Uekermünde, 1850
v. Bock, [W.], *Erinnerungen an eine große Zeit*, Berlin, 1913
Jahn, Gustav [editor], *Kamerad Hechel, 3rd edition*, Eisleben 1865
Kretzschmer, J. C., *Soldaten-, Kriegs- und Lagerleben. 2 vol.*, Danzig 1838.

von Rahden, Wilhelm, *Wanderungen eines alten Soldaten*. 1st part, Berlin 1846.

Rehtwisch [editor], *Aus dem Tagebuch eines Freiwilligen*. Leipzig 1910.

Renner, Karl, *Beiträge zur Rückerinnerung an die denkwürdigen Feldzüge der Preußen in den Jahren 1812 bis 1815*. Glogau 1829.

Riemann, Heinrich Arminius, *Der Unteroffizier im Regimente Colberg Sophia Dorothea Friederike Krüger*. Berlin 1865.

For uniform regulations, the standard sources are:

Ribbentrop, *Sammlung von Vorschriften, Anweisungen und sonstigen Aufsätzen über die Bekleidung bei der Königlich Preußischen Armee*, 2nd (revised) edition, Berlin, 1815

Mila, A, *Geschichte der Bekleidung und Ausrüstung der Königlich Preußischen Armee in den Jahren 1808 bis 1878*, Berlin, 1878

Pietsch, Paul, *Die Formations- und Uniformierungs-Geschichte des preußischen Heeres 1808-1914*, 2 vols, 2nd edition, Hamburg, 1963–66

Many regimental histories contain useful information on various aspects of soldiers' lives. All of them are listed in the following, comprehensive bibliography:

Mohr, Eike, *Heeres- und Truppengeschichte des Deutschen Reiches und seiner Länder 1806 bis 1918 – eine Bibliographie*, Osnabrück, 1989

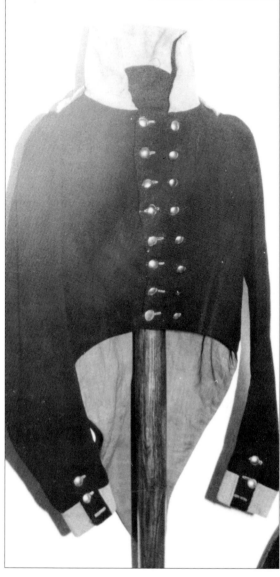

BELOW **A detail of the collar and shoulders. The very high collar is typical for the years around 1810. The shoulder straps on this uniform have buttonholes and can be unbuttoned.**

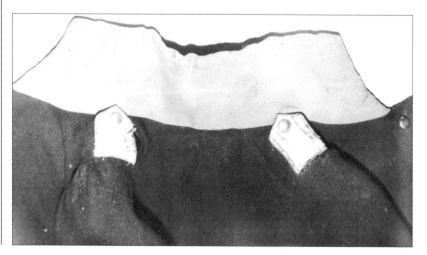

ABOVE **Officer's uniform of the 3. Ostpreußisches Infanterie-Regiment. The shoulder straps (46mm wide, 50mm long at the edges and 62 in the middle) are those of a Lieutenant after 18 June 1812, or those of a Kapitain before that date. The cuffs are 50mm high, cuff flaps are 100mm long and 38mm wide. In this example, the openings of the coat tail pockets lie below the pocket flaps. (Blüchermuseum Kaub)**

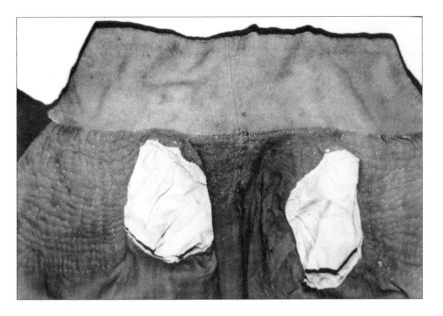

Inside view. The whole lining is red, note the stitches required to secure the padding in the chest.

# COLOUR PLATE COMMENTARY

### A: *FÜSILIER* OF THE *LEICHTES BATAILLON* OF THE *COLBERGSCHES INFANTERIE-REGIMENT*, DECEMBER 1808

On 26 August 1808 the *Colbergsches Infanterie-Regiment* was created from units which had taken part in the defence of the fortress of Colberg. The light battalion of this regiment

was formed from the *Füsilier-Bataillon von Möller*. Originally it had been organised in November 1806 by *Kapitain* von Möller under the name of *Pommersches Provisorisches Füsilier-Bataillon* (Pomeranian provisional *Füsilier* battalion: it comprised a few NCOs and soldiers of the depot of the *Westphälische* and the *Magdeburgische Füsilier-Brigade*, escaped Prussian prisoners of war who had rejoined the army and 100 new recruits from Pomerania. *Füsilier-Brigade* had been the denomination used in Prussia for the regiments of *Füsiliere* before 1808.

An *AKO* of 23 October 1808 introduced new uniforms for the whole army, but due to the financial exhaustion of the state the changes could not be immediatley implemented and many old uniforms and equipment or parts of it continued to be worn for some time. As a first step, on 6 August 1808 the King ordered that all the light batallions of the infantry regiments should receive the regular blue uniforms by 1 June 1809.

The soldier we see here still wears the basic uniform of the *Füsilier-Bataillon von Möller*.

The felt shako still bears the eagle, the emblem of the *Füsiliere* of the old army, of which they were particularly proud. It was replaced by the above-mentioned *AKO* of

Hans Karl Friedrich Franz von Below as *Oberst*, between 1808 and 1811. Born on 16 July 1764, he joined the infantry in 1780. On 17 September 1806, he was appointed commander of the *Infanterie-Regiment von Schöning* (No. 11), which became the *2. Ostpreußisches Infanterie-Regiment Prinz Heinrich* in 1808. In 1811 he was relieved of the command of his regiment in order to concentrate fully on his task as Brigadier (akin to an inspector, responsible for the military training of the units) of the East Prussian infantry regiments. In 1812, he commanded a brigade and, being no longer fit for active service, received his final dismission in 1815. He died in 1840. *Oberst* von Below was renowned as an excellent organisator.

23 October 1808 with the cockade with a white woollen clasp. This was not popular with many *Füsiliere*, but the King's will had to be obeyed. The former coloured pompon has already been replaced by the black and white national pompon.

The coat which in the 'old' army had been hooked together at the front has been made wider and is buttoned across the breast so that the crimson lapels can no longer be seen. Crimson was the distinctive colour of the *Westphälische Füsilier-Brigade* and was chosen for the *Füsilier-Bataillon von Möller* as well, together with the former's white metal buttons and eagle.

The belts for *Füsiliere* were as before, namely leather coated with a layer of black wax. The wide belt slung over the man's left shoulder to which the huge cartridge pouch is attached is typical for the infantry of the Prussian army before 1808. The three straps over the right shoulder belong to the calfskin pack, a linen breadbag and the tin water canteen.

The battalion carried British muskets, probably of the 'India Pattern', which is shown here. This man, as for many of his comrades throughout the infantry, does not carry a weapon at his side. The sabre would have been attached to the belt worn around the waist.

## Regulation muskets

Between 1808 and 1815, Prussian muskets of the models listed below ('M' stands for *Modell*) were still in use in the Prussian army. In addition, many foreign muskets were in use, namely British, Austrian, French, Swedish and Russian ones.

1  Infantry musket M 1780/87

Calibre: 18.6mm. Barrel length: 105.3cm. Overall length: 146.5cm. The lock is in the half-cock position, the pan closed. In this safety position, the musket cannot be fired – provided that the lock is not damaged. The flintstone is wrapped in paper to be screwed between the iron jaws of the cock. Instead of paper, cloth or leather could also be used for this purpose. However, these materials could start smouldering after firing, with the (albeit small) risk of premature ignition of the next charge. Therefore the flintstone was sometimes enclosed between pieces of lead instead: lead, however, was more expensive, whereas paper and cloth were much cheaper to obtain.

2  *Füsilier* musket M 1787

Calibre: 18.6mm. Barrel length: 93cm. Overall length: 133cm. The lock is fully cocked: pressing the trigger will cause the cock to spring forward, the flint hits the hammer, causing sparks to fly. The sparks ignite the powder in the pan, and via the touchhole, the powder in the barrel. The exploding powder charge propels the bullet forward.

3  Rifled sharpshooter musket M 1787

Calibre: 18.3mm. Eight grooves. Barrel length: 82.3cm. Overall length: 121cm. This rifle has a switchable sight for 150 paces (ca. 112m) and 300 paces (ca. 125m). Theoretically, after 1808 all the NCOs of the line infantry were to be equipped with this sharpshooter musket.

4  New Prussian musket M 1809

Calibre: 17.9mm. Barrel length: 104.6cm. Overall length: 143.5cm. The lock has been triggered. A musket would be stored in depot with the lock in this position, to prevent the springs wearing out in the course of time.

Major Bogislav Christian Karl von Kurnatowski, between 1808 and 1813. He was born on 3 April 1764. Having joined the infantry in 1779, in 1795 he was transferred to the *Füsilier-Bataillon* No. 11. In 1804, his regimental commander wrote of him 'Has some capabilities, but can't be relied on.' Nevertheless he took over command of his battalion in 1808, when it became the *Füsilier-Bataillon* of the *1. Ostpreußisches Infanterie-Regiment*. On 15 February 1810, he was appointed commander of this regiment's 1st battalion, and in 1814 he became the regimental commander. He died in 1826. The very dark collar (which should be brick red) is hard to explain. The distinctive colour of the *Füsilier-Bataillon* No. 11 had been light green. Unfortunately, the original from which this photograph is taken is black and white.

## Regulation sabres

Prussian sabres were of three types during this period. After the war of 1806/07, the Prussian army was short of these weapons: it was decided that NCOs, drummers, buglers and musicians should receive them first, then grenadiers and those men who had received honorary sabre tassels. With the huge expansion of the army in 1813, sabres were again in short supply.

5  'Old Prussian' sabre M 1715

The length of the blade of this model had been reduced to about 63cm in 1744. Often it was even less, as these sabres were in use for many years and were resharpened from time to time.

**6** *Füsilier* sabre M 1787

Length of the blade: 48cm. This type of sabre was the regulation sabre for the *Füsilier* battalions throughout the Napoleonic Wars. An AKO of 23 January 1819 allowed the Füsilier battalions to choose between this sabre and the standard infantry sabre.

**7** New Prussian sabre M 1816

Length of the blade: 60cm. This model was introduced after the Napoleonic Wars, making use of tens of thousands of captured sabres: it closely resembles the French 1801-type sabre.

## Regulation sabre belts

There were two new patterns of sabre belt post 1808:

**8** Sabre belt for *Grenadiere* and *Musketiere*

This was introduced on 10 December 1810. Normally, this belt was worn over the shoulder, but on parades it could be worn around the hips, as had been the norm in the 'old Prussian' army of pre-1806. The belts for *Grenadiere* and *Musketiere* were of leather whitened with chalk.

**9** Sabre belt for *Füsiliere*

**The 2nd battalion of the *Leib-Infanterie-Regiment* passing General von Yorck the day after it stormed the village of Wartenburg (3 October 1813), in a late 19th-century drawing by W. Camphausen. The general, nicknamed by his soldiers 'der alte Isegrim' ('the old grumbler'), was well known for being slow to praise, but on this occasion he took off his hat and spoke the words: 'This is the brave battalion, for which the whole world must have respect.'**

This sabre belt could only be worn over the shoulder. This new manner of wearing the sabre was introduced by the *AKO* of 23 October 1808. In this, the king ordered that bayonets should be worn in this belt, but it became normal for Prussian soldiers to carry them fixed to their muskets.

## B: A GROUP OF SOLDIERS OF THE *FÜSILIER-BATAILLON* OF THE *COLBERGSCHES INFANTERIE-REGIMENT* ON SHOOTING EXERCISE, SUMMER 1811

On 1 December 1809, the light battalions of the infantry regiments were renamed *Füsilier* battalions.

In 1811 the battalion received Prussian M 1809 muskets. In this illustration, the *Unteroffizier* has put his rifled sharpshooter musket M 1787 on the ground and has taken the musket of one of the men, explaining why it has misfired.

All the soldiers wear the regulation uniform introduced in 1808. White collar and cuffs (identifying the province of Pomerania) in combination with red shoulder straps are the distinctions of the *Colbergsches Infanterie-Regiment*.

The black belts, plain cartridge pouches without decoration and the shakos with a cockade on the front indicate that they are *Füsiliere*. We can tell that they belong to the 2nd company of the *Füsilier* battalion by the colours of their sword tassels (cf. plate H, No 42).

The *Unteroffizier* can be identified by the golden lace on the front and bottom of his collar and around the cuffs. In addition, he has gold lace around the top of his shako instead of the white woollen one of the men. The clasp on the cockade is of brass, whereas the men's is of white

Contemporary print of a field service attended by the Prussian King to his left, his son, (later Friedrich Wilhelm IV) and his guards on 1 September 1813. This service was held in order to give praise for the victory at Kulm. At the end of September 1813, the King ordered daily morning and evening prayers to be said in his army.

woollen lace. Another distiction of his rank is a black and white sword tassel on a white band with a black stripe on each side (cf. plate H, No 47).

NCOs carried their cartridge pouch on a belt above the lowest four buttons of their uniform coat. Because their main role in battle was supervision, their cartridge pouch was quite small compared to those of the men.

Following the *AKO* of 23 October 1808, the calfskin knapsacks with an inner cloth lining replaced the packs worn on the left hip. They were large enough to carry eight pounds of clothing and equipment in them, as well as a man's bread ration. The financial situation of the state did not allow for all the old sidepacks to be replaced at once, so many of these were modified by attaching two slings, allowing them to be worn over both shoulders. As they were much smaller than the new pattern, bread had to be carried in an extra bread bag made from linen, which was issued in case of mobilisation of the unit.

In 1810 the two shoulder straps of the knapsack were connected by a leather strap across the chest. It seems that this was not put immediately into practice in all battalions. As late as 31 December 1813, the men of the *Füsilier* battalion of the *2. Garde-Regiment zu Fuß*, which had been the *Füsilier* battalion of the *Leib-Infanterie-Regiment* before 19 June 1813, were ordered to purchase a small iron buckle at their own expense for the chest straps 'which the regiment will receive shortly'.

On 21 November 1815 the knapsacks received new straps, 1.5 *Zoll* (4.6cm) wide, replacing those of 1 *Zoll* (2.6cm) width carried previously.

## C: WAKING THE SOLDIERS OF THE *FÜSILIER-BATAILLON* OF THE *COLBERGSCHES INFANTERIE-REGIMENT*, SPRING 1812

In this scene, an *Unteroffizier* is rousing his men in the morning, as best he can.

The underwear of common men and soldiers of the Napoleonic Period consisted of a single shirt, which went down to the knees. This shirt also served as a nightshirt. No underpants, shorts or the like were worn. The shirt had a button at the neck and sleeve-links made from wood or bone.

Due to the prevailing fashion in the years around 1810, which demanded a high waist, the trousers had to be worn with suspenders. The buttons of the front flap were not visible when the waistcoat or the uniform was worn, though worn instead. We know of several complaints by the commander of the *Füsilier* battalion of the *2. Garde-Regiment zu Fuß*, Major Freiherr von Quadt und Hüchtenbruck, in the first half of 1814, regarding men who wore coloured neckcloths or none at all whilst marching. Finally, in an order to the battalion on 15 June 1814, he succeeded in putting an end to this practice by making the company commanders responsible: 'the gentlemen company commanders will be so kind to insist with all strictness that all NCOs, *Spielleute* and *Füsiliere* will wear neckstocks or neckcloths'.

After 1808, NCOs in the infantry continued to carry privately purchased canes of wood as an unofficial symbol of their rank. On 12 February 1813, the carrying of canes was forbidden for newly appointed NCOs only, and on departure into the field established NCOs were also instructed to leave their canes in garrison. Some no doubt would have realised that they might not return to collect them.

### D: THE *2. POMMERSCHES RESERVE-BATAILLON* FORMS AN ATTACK COLUMN FROM THE LINE NEAR THE VILLAGE OF GRABOW, 12 MAY 1813

On this day the blockading corps in front of the fortress of Stettin pushed back a sally by the French garrison. The *2. Pommersches Reserve-Bataillon*, being part of this blockading corps, is forming an attack column: the 1st and 8th *Zug*, who originally stood at the right and left wing of the battalion, have almost completed their move into position. The battalion's casualties for this engagement will be one man dead, several lightly wounded, and one man severely wounded – *Lieutenant* von Puttkamer.

This battalion had been formed in January 1813 near the Pomeranian town of *Cörlin* from *Krümper* and *Kantonisten* under the name *2. Miliz-Bataillon* (2nd Militia Battalion). Following an order of 2 February 1813, 8 *Unteroffiziere*, 40 *Füsiliere* and 1 *Spielmann* were to be transferred from a line battalion to each of the 8 Pomeranian *Miliz-Bataillone*. The *2. Miliz-Bataillon* received its cadre from the *Füsilier-Bataillon* of the *Colbergsches Infanterie-Regiment*. The battalion changed its name in February 1813, when all the *Miliz-Bataillone* were renamed *Reserve-Bataillone*.

Due to the difficulties in equipping so many new battalions at once, an *AKO* of 20 December 1812 decreed that the men of the newly raised battalions should receive a simplified uniform, much cheaper than the regulation uniform. This was the so-called '*Krümper-Uniform*' and comprised jackets and trousers of grey cloth. Men were allowed to wear their own civilian trousers if there was a lack of the official ones. Head dress consisted mainly of caps of grey cloth with a stripe in the provincial colour – white for Pomerania.

*General* von Borstell had ordered on 30 January 1813 that in the Pomeranian *Miliz-Bataillone* the number of the batallion should be attached in grey cloth to these stripes. Shoulder straps were of grey cloth, NCOs should have them made of blue cloth with the number of the battalion on it. The cadres who had been transferred from the line battalions continued to wear the regulation uniforms they had brought with them.

The Pomeranian battalions were armed with 'old Prussian' and Swedish muskets. Each man carried an 'old Prussian' cartridge pouch, but only a few were lucky enough to possess

**A shako of British origin, in short, a felt cone with leather bands around the top and bottom, leather peak and chinstraps. It has a white metal horn and a dark green woollen plume. (Wehrgeschichtliches Museum Rastatt)**

in some inspection reports of the Napoleonic period we are told that several men had come to parade with their front flaps of their trousers unbuttoned. It was the duty of the *Unteroffizier* to ensure that his men were clean and properly dressed.

For fastening the tight (and therefore often hated) gaiters, the men usually made use of a short cord which was fed through the buttonhole and fastened around the base of the button.

Neckstocks were regarded as an essential part of proper civilian or military dress throughout the Napoleonic Wars, as well as before and after. The regulation neckstock was of black cloth as depicted here. Sometimes black neckcloths were

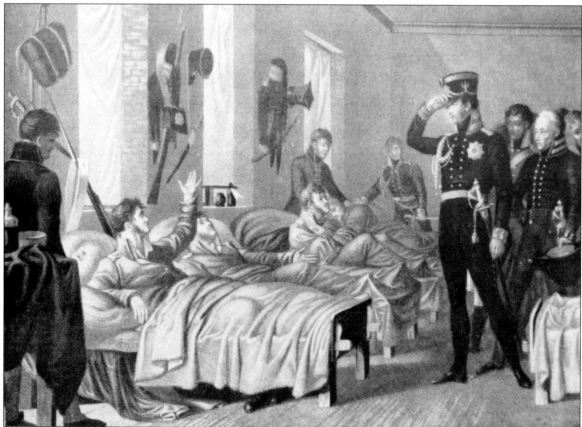

Prince Wilhelm von Preußen in 1814, aged 17, *Kapitain* in the *1. Garde-Regiment zu Fuß*, from a contemporary painting by Karl Steuben. Second son of the King, he succeeded his brother and became King of Prussia in 1861 and Emperor of the united Germany in 1871. The white band around the left upper arm was introduced in early 1814 as a common military badge for all the Allied troops, but only few Prussian units actually wore it.

*Musketiere* of the *Leib-Infanterie-Regiment* re-enactment group, demonstrating skirmishing in winter. Usually, skirmishers went out in pairs, firing alternately. After the first had fired, the second waited until the first had reloaded, so that the two together always had one shot in reserve.

ABOVE OPPOSITE **View of the Ranstädter gate in Leipzig on 20 October 1813. Most of the dead have been already stripped of their clothes, but some things worth looting can still be seen.**

BELOW OPPOSITE **King Friedrich Wilhelm III visiting the military hospital in Bautzen, in a contemporary print by Jügel after a drawing by Ludwig Wolf. This military hospital is extremely well presented and the wounded have a lot of space. Conditions were usually much worse.**

a knapsack, the others had to use linen bags instead. Only one man in three or four had cooking equipment.

On 20 February 1813 the NCOs of the Pomeranian reserve batallions received greatcoats and haversacks as well as Prussian *Füsilier* muskets, but the ordinary soldiers of the *2. Reserve-Bataillon* had to wait until the beginning of March to receive their greatcoats. They were comparatively lucky to receive them all in one go: the 801 men of the *5. Reserve-Bataillon* only received 200 at the beginning, with another 400 following on 12 March.

On 27 April the battalion had to dispatch one of its four companies (without the officers and NCOs) as replacements for the army: the company was re-formed with raw recruits – and had to be newly equipped!

Different ideas and concepts of how to organise the newly raised battalions were competing with each other at this time. During the month of May, the *2. Pommersches Reserve-Bataillon* was first renamed *Colbergsches Füsilier-Reserve-Bataillon*, but a few days later this was changed to *4. Reserve-Bataillon Colbergschen Regiment*.

**55**

## E: THE *FÜSILIER-BATAILLON* OF THE *9. RESERVE-INFANTERIE-REGIMENT* SETS UP CAMP CLOSE TO SCHADEWALDE NEAR THE FORTRESS OF WITTENBERG, 13 SEPTEMBER 1813

Being assigned as a reserve to the besieging corps of Wittenberg, the *9. Reserve-Infanterie-Regiment* expected to stay in the assigned area for a few days, and so the men built huts for shelter. The roof of the hut shown here has already been finished and is put on the side wall structures. The next step will be to construct the walls from interwoven willow-twigs, bushes and straw.

With the *AKO* of 1 July 1813, the *4. Reserve-Bataillon Colbergschen Regiment* had become the *3. Bataillon* of the *9. Reserve-Infanterie-Regiment*. Within six months, it had changed names five times. It was informed about this new change in mid-July, and the new regiment was united for the first time on 7 August 1813 in Berlin. By mid-August 1813, the 3rd battalion was already named *Füsilier-Bataillon*, though officially it received this denomination only following an *AKO* of 6 September 1815.

In mid-July, the battalion had exchanged its uniforms for 'rather good' British uniforms, which can be seen here, they received British greatcoats of grey cloth, black belts, shirts, shoes and clothes brushes as well. By 1 June 1813, it had been equipped with British muskets, giving its 'old Prussian' and Swedish muskets to the *Landwehr*.

It was the firm belief of most of the soldiers who had received British uniforms that the cargo of two ships with uniform supplies for Spain and Prussia had been swapped in error, and that someone in Spain was marching around in 'their' Prussian uniform. The truth was that the British government had not bothered to provide their Prussian allies with uniforms that followed the Prussian regulations.

There are two descriptions of these green British uniforms. One is given by von Mila in his work on Prussian uniforms and is taken from a drawing by his father, who saw the *9. Reserve-Infanterie-Regiment* in 1813 in Berlin and, according to his son, 'had a sharp eye for such details':

Dark green uniform coats, of the same cut as in the first two battalions [who wore 'long uniforms with wide tails'], black collars, black Swedish cuffs, no turnbacks, black shoulder straps with wings of the same colour, in the front three rows of white buttons, extending their distance towards the shoulders. Green trousers with black gaiters. Shakos as in the 1st battalion ['black conical shakos without a peak at the back, front peak without a rim, black chinstraps'], but in front instead of the round plate a white bugle, above it the cockade, on the top a dark green oval pompon. The other parts as in the 1st battalion ['cartridge pouch with black belt,

**Contemporary print of a Prussian camp. The huts are partly made from wooden planks. The men off duty wear their grey field caps with a stripe in the provincial colour around the bottom instead of their heavy shakos. Being in the open without a hat was generally considered improper dress in the Napoleonic period, though, obviously, there were exceptions.**

knapsack of light brown leather, muskets with bayonets, no sabres'] – Officers dark blue uniforms as in the 1st battalion [the regulation uniform], black collars and cuffs without piping, red shoulder straps with a yellow '9', the rest like the officers of the other battalions ['Prussian shakos with yellow lace around the top, cockade and clasp. Black trousers with red side seam and yellow buttons. Sabres as per the *Füsiliere* officers'].

The description in the regimental history is slightly different: 'Green uniforms, collar, cuffs, wings, turnbacks black, belts of the same colour. NCOs received woollen sashes. The officers wore the uniform of the Prussian line regiments with Pomeranian distinctions, i.e. white collars and cuffs. On the shoulder straps, they had a number made in gold thread. Grey overcoats, greatcoats and trousers of the same colour. The latter had red side seams and on each side a row of yellow buttons going down to the feet. In addition, officers had covered field caps, sashes, a sabre or sword.'

According to an order of 12 August 1813 the NCOs were allowed to put on their woollen sashes only if especially ordered to do so by the regimental commander, for example on parades.

According to an order by *General-Lieutenant* von Bülow of 10 August 1813, the white collars of the officers of *9. Reserve-Infanterie-Regiment* were to be covered with a collar in the colour of the collars of the men, in order not to attract fire from enemy skirmishers. These overcollars could be removed on parades.

The *9. Reserve-Infanterie-Regiment* belonged to the 6th Prussian Brigade commanded by *Oberst* (after 21 August 1813, *General-Major*) von Krafft. According to accounts by officers after the Napoleonic Wars, it constantly experienced worse supply, and poorer quartering and camp placement than the line regiment in this brigade, the *Colbergsches Infanterie-*

**Prussian soldiers crossing a river at full moon in 1813, in a contemporary print by Ludwig Wolf. Note the distinctive outline of Prussian line infantry: their rolled greatcoats slung over the left shoulder and the waxed cloth cover on the shako with a small elevation at the front caused by the black and white pompon. (Kupferstichkabinett Berlin)**

**Return of a *Lieutenant* from war in 1814, a popular contemporary print. In the background his valet is holding his horse. The officer wears the epaulette introduced on 28 December 1813. Staff officers and *Kapitains* would have two rows of silver fringes.**

*Regiment.* In times of general need, it is likely that commanders tried to preserve their more experienced units first.

## F: THE *FÜSILIER-BATAILLON* OF THE 9. *RESERVE-INFANTERIE-REGIMENT* SKIRMISHING ON THE MORNING OF THE BATTLE OF LAON, ON THE SLOPE ABOVE THE VILLAGE ARDON, 9 MARCH 1814

A company surgeon has installed himself in one of the vineyards. Further down the slope, the line of the supporting detachment for the skirmishers can be seen. Thanks to the fog which lasted until noon, the two battalions of the *9. Reserve-Infanterie-Regiment* who were mainly engaged in skirmishing lost only 4 men and suffered 19 wounded on this day.

From 15 to 19 November 1814, the regiment stayed in the town of Münster. With the help of civilian craftsmen, they spent the time repairing their clothing and equipment, ready for the winter campaign.

By the beginning of January 1814, the *Füsilier-Bataillon* had been reduced to 400 men. In the course of January, the regiment received 333 reinforcements, who were distributed to the companies. The regimental history notes that the uniforms of the new men had the uniform distinctions of many different regiments, unfortunately no more detail is provided. The uniforms of the reinforcements were always taken from stock at hand, there was no question of selecting uniforms matching those of the destination unit.

In the winter campaign of 1814, greatcoats were generally worn, which covered up the diversity and the ragged state of the uniforms beneath them.

The uniform of the company surgeons had been prescribed on 15 November 1808 as: 'dark blue uniform with one row of the same buttons as are worn by the regiment. Collar, cuffs and lining of the uniform of blue colour, but all three with piping in the colour of the regiment's collar. This piping is to be found on collar and cuffs, down the front of the uniform, on the pocket flaps and on the turnbacks.' The shoulder straps were also identical to those of the regiment.

## G: MEN OF THE *FÜSILIER-BATAILLON* OF THE 21. *INFANTERIE-REGIMENT* DURING THE STORMING OF MEDY-BAS, 15 SEPTEMBER 1815

This illustration shows what were probably some of the last shots fired in the Napoleonic Wars. The town in the valley at the foot of the fortress Montmédy was stormed by 400 men of the *21. Infanterie-Regiment* and 100 infantrymen from Sachsen-Weimar in the early morning hours of 15 September.

**Kaiser Alexander Grenadier-Regiment in 1816, contemporary engraving by Friedrich Jügel after a drawing by Ludwig Wolf. To the left a Grenadier of one of the two Grenadier-Bataillone, to the right a Grenadier of the Füsilier-Bataillon. Note the folding of the greatcoat into a flat band, which had already become fashionable in 1815. The wide belts of the knapsack were introduced on 21 November 1815.**

The approach of the attackers was noticed, but nevertheless some Prussians managed to climb the walls and open the gates for the other troops. Four of the attackers were severly wounded. The town was bombarded from the main fortress during the next day and had to be abandoned, but the fortress itself capitulated on 19 September 1815.

On 25 March 1815, the *9. Reserve-Infanterie-Regiment* was renamed *21. Infanterie-Regiment*, but got to know its new name only on 21 April 1815 in its quarters in Belgium, as orders had been issued by the King at the congress in distant Vienna.

During the period from 14 May to 1 July 1814, the regiment stayed in the town of Ghent in Flanders. Here again, clothing and equipment were repaired with the assistance of civilian craftsmen, and reinforcements restored the regiment's strength. In July 1814, the regiment received a small supply of new uniforms. The collars were probably changed according to the new pattern at this point: they were lower and closed at the front.

In October 1814, the regiment received trousers of blue cloth as well as 132 new greatcoats. One month later, 487 uniforms arrived which still had yet to be provided with new collars. Most of the uniforms of British origin were altered according to the Prussian pattern, so that finally, in December 1814, the whole regiment wore blue uniforms with white collars and cuffs and red shoulder straps. All the green uniforms of the *Füsilier-Bataillon* had been replaced with blue ones.

The 'weak spot' was the British shako. In order to give it a more Prussian-like appearance, it received a wax cloth cover, the wide Prussian top was simulated with cardboard and the whole stuffed out with padding. The results were not always convincing.

In August 1815, during the blockade of the fortress Givet, uniforms and equipment were again repaired. During this period, the first white linen gaiter trousers were produced for the regiment, to be worn on parades.

The regiment's appearance was still not unified though. In this illustration, we see altered French uniforms, and a mixture of British, Prussian and French knapsacks. Most of the uniforms and trousers are old, worn and faded, but patched and repaired with care.

The storming party is led by an engineer officer. He wears his overcoat and can be identified by his black velvet collar.

## H: FELDWEBEL OF THE FÜSILIER-BATAILLON OF THE 21. INFANTERIE-REGIMENT, OCTOBER 1815

This *Feldwebel* (sergeant major) wears a uniform according to the latest regulations, apart from his red shoulder straps, which have not yet been replaced by light blue ones.

His rank as an NCO is indicated by the gold lace around the collar and cuffs and the brass clasp. The band around the top of the shako has already been removed by an order of 13 December 1812. The *Feldwebel* is distinguished from the *Unteroffiziere* by his silver officer's sword tassle.

NCOs in this regiment were particulary proud of their white leather gloves, which had been delivered to them at the end of 1814.

Inside the collar and overlapping it, the *Feldwebel* wears another small collar which serves to protect the collar from getting dirty. On 6 March 1815, the men of the *2. Garde-Regiment zu Fuß* were allowed to purchase red protective

collars (at their own expense) and wear them for exercise and on guard duty, but not on parades. These collars are sometimes depicted on contemporary drawings of different regiments.

The brass medal this man wears on his breast is the commemorative medal that every active participant in the campaigns from 1813 to 1815 received. It was supported by an orange band edged with two white stripes, the latter having a black lining on each side.

## Regimental distinctions in 1815

With the *AKO* of 23 October 1808 the regiments were distinguished by their provincial colour on collars and cuffs (brick red for East Prussia, white for Pomerania, crimson for West Prussia, red for Brandenburg, yellow for Silesia) and the colour of seniority within their province on their shoulder straps (white for the 1st, red for the 2nd, yellow for the 3rd and light blue for the 4th regiment).

The *AKO* of 25 March 1815 extended this system by prescribing the following combination of collar and shoulder straps for the 32 line infantry regiments, some of which were newly formed. The cuffs were of the same colour as the collar. These regimental distinctions did not last long: on 9 February 1816 a new system was introduced and all the regiments received red collars.

Though the first 12 regiments were officially numbered and ranked according to their seniority, in reports and other documents these regiments were always referred to just by their provincial designation. The two regiments with honorific titles, the *Leib-Infanterie-Regiment* [King's Own Infantry Regiment] and the *Colbergsches Infanterie-Regiment*, which had been formed from the victorious garrison defending the fortress Colberg in 1807, were exceptions. They were never referred to by any provincial designation.

A common misconception, found in many publications on the Prussian army is that the other regiments were given provincial designations too when they were renamed or formed in 1815. In fact, these new regiments did not receive any provincial designation until the *AKO* of 5 November 1816. For example, the *13. Infanterie-Regiment* was not named the *13. Infanterie-Regiment (1. Westphälisches)* until that very day. With the same *AKO*, the first 12 regiments included their numbers in their names, e.g. the *1. Pommersches Infanterie-Regiment* was named *2. Infanterie-Regiment (1. Pommersches)* from that date onwards.

1   1. Ostpreußisches Infanterie-Regiment Prinz Carl von Mecklenburg-Strelitz

On 20 or 21 October 1813, after the Battle of Leipzig, the Prince of Mecklenburg-Strelitz, who commanded the 2nd Prussian Infantry Brigade, was rewarded by being made *Regiments-Chef* of the *1. Ostpreußisches Infanterie-Regiment*. The regiment's designation in the army lists was then changed to *1. Ostpreußisches Infanterie-Regiment Prinz Carl von Mecklenburg-Strelitz*.

2   1. Pommersches Infanterie-Regiment

3   2. Ostpreußisches Infanterie-Regiment Prinz Heinrich

The King had given permission in a note to the AKO of 14 November 1808, that those regiments which still had an 'active' Regiments-Chef could retain his name in their regimental designation. However, this practice was discontinued after 29 December 1809. After that date only

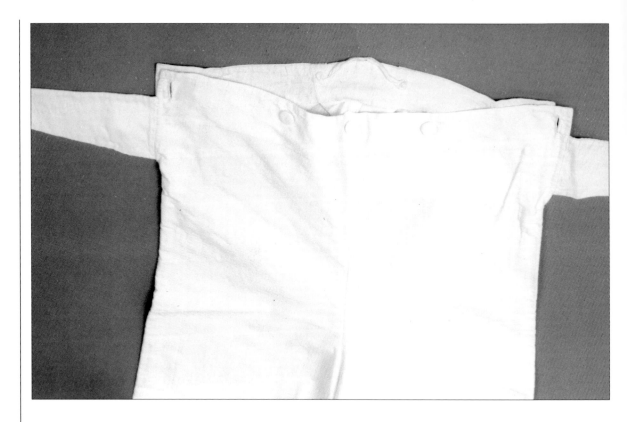

ABOVE  **Detail of the front of a Prussian officer's gaiters. Following the Russian pattern, this type of white linen trouser was introduced for the Prussian infantry with the *AKO* of 7 April 1815. In 1814/15, the front flap of the Prussian military trousers became wider than before and now reached up to the side seams. (Wehrgeschichtliches Museum Rastatt)**

BELOW  **Rear view. The two linen straps on the back were fastened with a buckle and served to tighten the trousers at the waist. In addition, the gaiter trousers were kept in place by braces, which were fastened to buttons.**

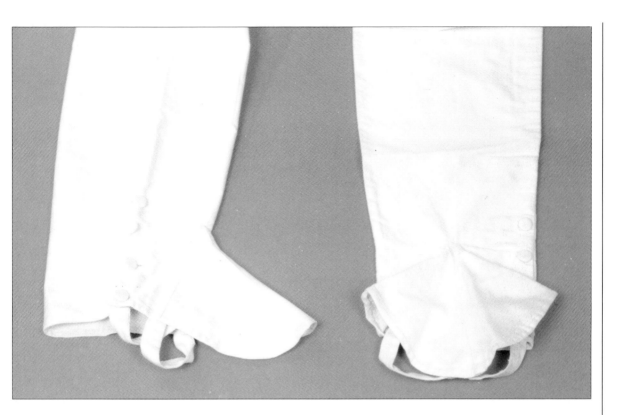

**Detail of the gaiters. The linen strap beneath was not sewn on: one end had a button hole and the other was fixed with a needle.**

members of the Royal family were still honoured in this way. In the infantry, the only regiment distinguished in this way was the 2. Ostpreußisches Infanterie-Regiment Prinz Heinrich, whose Regiments-Chef since 8 March 1807 had been Prince Heinrich, younger brother of the king.

4    3. Ostpreußisches Infanterie-Regiment

5    4. Ostpreußisches Infanterie-Regiment

6    1. Westpreußisches Infanterie-Regiment

7    2. Westpreußisches Infanterie-Regiment

8    Leib-Infanterie-Regiment
In order to comply with the restriction to ten line regiments in the Treaty of Paris, the French government had been told the Leib-Infanterie-Regiment was part of the Royal Guard. However, its status within the Prussian army always remained that of a regular line infantry regiment.

9    Colbergsches Infanterie-Regiment
The AKO of 1 July 1813 ordered that the 1. and 2. Garde-Regiment zu Fuß should rank before the line regiments and they were removed from the seniority list. Therefore the four regiments that had hitherto been numbered 9 to 12 in the army list stepped up a level each, now occupying numbers 8 to 11.

10    1. Schlesisches Infanterie-Regiment

11    2. Schlesisches Infanterie-Regiment

12    2. Brandenburgisches Infanterie-Regiment

This regiment was newly formed with the AKO of 1 July 1813. The 1st regiment from the province of Brandenburg was the Leib-Infanterie-Regiment, though it was never referred to by this provincial name.

13    13. Infanterie-Regiment
The AKOs of 7 and 25 March 1815 renamed the 1. to 12. Reserve-Infanterie-Regiment as the 13. to 24. Infanterie-Regiment and created the 25. to 31. Infanterie-Regiment, mainly from existing volunteer and foreign units that had been formed in 1813.

14    14. Infanterie-Regiment

15    15. Infanterie-Regiment
This regiment changed its collars from brick red to yellow in May 1815.

16    16. Infanterie-Regiment

17    17. Infanterie-Regiment

18    18. Infanterie-Regiment
In June 1815 this regiment was about to change its collars to the new colour. When the campaign started, a part of the regiment had to move out in uniforms without collars. In some English publications on the Prussian army the story is reported that the men of this regiment tore off their collars in order to march to the battlefield more easily, and that for this act, the regiment was rewarded with the right to wear rose-red collars by the King. However, this regiment had already received rose-red as its distinctive colour by the above-mentioned AKO of 25 March, showing this story to be pure fiction.

19    19. Infanterie-Regiment

20    20. Infanterie-Regiment

| | |
|---|---|
| 21 | 21. Infanterie-Regiment |
| 22 | 22. Infanterie-Regiment |
| 23 | 23. Infanterie-Regiment |
| 24 | 24. Infanterie-Regiment |
| 25 | 25. Infanterie-Regiment |
| 26 | 26. Infanterie-Regiment |
| 27 | 27. Infanterie-Regiment |
| 28 | 28. Infanterie-Regiment |
| 29 | 29. Infanterie-Regiment |
| 30 | 30. Infanterie-Regiment |
| 31 | 31. Infanterie-Regiment |
| 32 | 32. Infanterie-Regiment |

This regiment was to be formed from troops acquired from Saxon territory at the Congress of Vienna. However, after the mutiny of the Saxon units in Liège in May 1815, on 5 June 1815 the regiment was ordered to be drawn from three Landwehr battalions instead. These three battalions were not united until 25 November 1815.

Company tassels

The privates' tassels in the regiment differed among the 14 companies. An AKO of 14 November 1808 prescribed the following arrangement, which lasted until 28 April 1818:

| | |
|---|---|
| 33 | 1st company |
| 34 | 2nd company |
| 35 | 3rd company |
| 36 | 4th company |
| 37 | 5th company |
| 38 | 6th company |
| 39 | 7th company |
| 40 | 8th company |
| 41 | 1st Füsilier company |
| 42 | 2nd Füsilier company |
| 43 | 3rd Füsilier company |
| 44 | 4th Füsilier company |
| 45 | 1st company of Grenadiere |

In the Leib-Grenadier-Bataillon, which consisted of four grenadier companies, the tassels of the 1st and 3rd company as well as those of the 2nd and 4th company were identical. When the six grenadier battalions were reorganised into Grenadier-Regimenter in October 1814, they received the same tassels as the other infantry regiments.

| | |
|---|---|
| 46 | 2nd company of Grenadiere |

Due to an error in von Mila's work, the colours for the slider and ring of the 2nd company of Grenadiere are often given wrongly as mixed black and white instead of plain black.

| | |
|---|---|
| 47 | The Unteroffizier's tassel |
| 48 | Honorary tassel for privates |

By an AKO of 17 March 1809, those privates who had been in active service in the army in 1807 at the date of the peace treaty were allowed to wear the Unteroffizier's tassel, but on a plain white band only.

OPPOSITE *Musketier of the 1. Pommersches Infanterie-Regiment* in the uniform prescribed by the *AKO of 9 February 1816*, in a contemporary engraving by Friedrich Jügel after a drawing by Ludwig Wolf. This is the parade dress worn by the Prussian infantry after the 1815 campaign, apart from the modern facing colours and the wide belts.

# INDEX

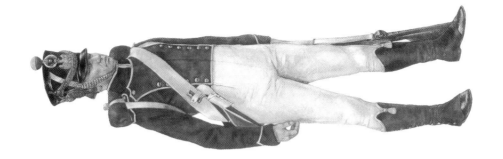

# FIND OUT MORE ABOUT OSPREY

❏ Please send me the latest listing of Osprey's publications

❏ I would like to subscribe to Osprey's e-mail newsletter

Title/rank _____

Name _____

Address _____

_____

_____

Postcode/zip _____ state/country _____

e-mail _____

I am interested in:

❏ Ancient world
❏ Medieval world
❏ 16th century
❏ 17th century
❏ 18th century
❏ Napoleonic
❏ 19th century

❏ American Civil War
❏ World War I
❏ World War II
❏ Modern warfare
❏ Military aviation
❏ Naval warfare

Please send to:

**USA & Canada**:
Osprey Direct USA, c/o MBI Publishing, P.O. Box 1,
729 Prospect Avenue, Osceola, WI 54020

**UK, Europe and rest of world**:
Osprey Direct UK, P.O. Box 140, Wellingborough,
Northants, NN8 2FA, United Kingdom

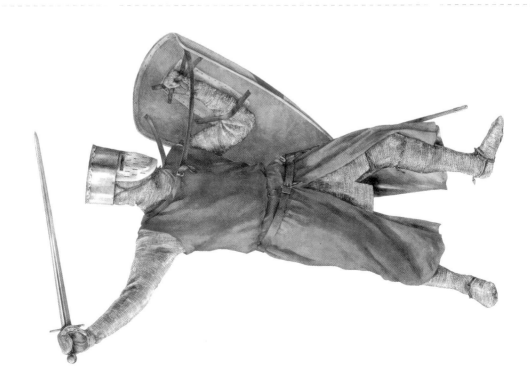

## OSPREY
### PUBLISHING

www.ospreypublishing.com

call our telephone hotline
for a free information pack

USA & Canada: 1-800-826-6600
UK, Europe and rest of world call:
+44 (0) 1933 443 863

**Young Guardsman**
Figure taken from *Warrior 22:*
*Imperial Guardsman 1799–1815*
Published by Osprey
Illustrated by Richard Hook

**Knight, c.1190**
Figure taken from *Warrior 1: Norman Knight 950 – 1204 AD*
Published by Osprey
Illustrated by Christa Hook

POSTCARD